SATURN

Spiritual Master, Spiritual Friend

Robert Wilkinson

First Published in 2016 by
Fifth Ray Publishing
Austin, Texas

Copyright © Robert Wilkinson
All rights reserved. No part of this publication may be reproduced or transmitted in any form or by any means, electronic or mechanical, including photocopying, recording, or by any information storage and retrieval system, without permission in writing from the author. Reviewers may quote brief passages.

Library of Congress Control Number: 2016914700
CreateSpace Independent Publishing Platform,
North Charleston, SC

Wilkinson, Robert
    Saturn: Spiritual Master, Spiritual Friend / Robert Wilkinson
    ISBN: 978-1-940751-03-0   2016
    1. Astrology   2. Body, Mind, Spirit

Fifth Ray Publishing
Austin, Texas

Comprehensive, engaging and rich, "Saturn: Spiritual Master, Spiritual Friend," is destined to become a classic and THE authoritative tome on the celestial task-master. First rate astrologer and gifted author Robert Wilkinson takes us on a journey to the revered Lord of Karma that leaves the reader fully informed and up-to-speed on every facet of the stylish and stern three-ringed planet. Much in the way that a student or seeker might align with a wise teacher and mentor, Wilkinson encourages astrologers of all ages to fall in love with and make friends with the "boss," liking Saturn more than you did before. A must read.
-Shelley L. Ackerman, New York, NY

"Saturn - Spiritual Master, Spiritual Friend' is not only an accessible astrological book but a gentle treatise on our evolutionary unfolding. Through exploring the meaning and cycles of Saturn, its links to the progressed Moon and connection to dharma and karma, Robert Wilkinson illuminates Old Father Time as both spiritual gatekeeper and honoured master. Saturn, as representative of our higher self, challenges us to move past limitations in order to fulfill our divine potential, opening the gateway to oneness with all that is. This book reveals the wise soul of Saturn whose teachings instruct us towards our own spiritual mastery. A beautifully composed and luminous text which takes our understanding of Saturn to the next level.
-Leah Whitehorse, UK

Robert Wilkinson's web columns are alternatively authoritative and sensitive, and occasionally outspoken at social injustice. They also focus on astrological aspects, techniques, historic events, and the overall picture of specific transits. Many call him "Professor Robert." Open this book's pages and you'll find a deeply caring, and understanding, paternal voice - enough to tempt you to call him "Papa Robert!" He makes handling Saturn's lesson look easy. Walking through transits and progressions with compassion, empathy, and you, he introduces you to Old Man Saturn as Father Time, Friend, and Sage. When you're finished with Chapter 1, don't be surprised if you really do feel like you've bathed in "the ocean of Divine Forgiveness."

Robert's masterful approach with reader-friendly text offers a *kaffeeklatsch* or a comfort zone for sitting and listening to him, and you'll know you've entered that very special world, Saturn! "It's all part of learning how to be 'perfectly human,' knowing what we can take responsibility for, and what we cannot," he says. Robert describes this journey from fear to the Hero's Journey and beyond to the very last page--your awareness of your Oneness. Here you discover you've met Saturn in ways you've never before thought possible. Whether you've experienced your first or even second Saturn return, this book guides you to the Saturn cycles. Experienced astrologer or student, the time for this book is now! - Michelle Young, NY

This book is a much needed gem for our world right now. It contains the key to unlocking the mystery of Saturn's influence in our lives, and opens the door to understanding Saturn's energy and how to use it for our highest good. Robert has a wonderful knack for breaking down deep, complicated subjects into words for everyday people. I love this book and it is greatly needed as we move through these times!
- Gayle McClellan Powell, Los Angeles, CA

Just as everyone has a bottle of aspirin in their medicine chest, so should everyone have Robert's new book "Saturn – Spiritual Master Spiritual Friend" in their bookcase. Chapter Four is my favorite as it clearly explains how Dharma and various types of Karma manifest, and provides valuable insights on how to get through life's ups and downs.
- Felipe Gonzales, Guatemala

"Saturn: Spiritual Master, Spiritual Friend" is a rich, multilayered book that rewards reading and re-reading, unfolding new insights each time.
- Kurt Madison, Spokane, WA

Many things have been written about Saturn, usually warning about all the things you better have together before the "whip comes down." Robert offers us an entirely new spiritual perspective on Saturn, and there are many places where it seems as if he is speaking directly to the reader soul to soul. The Ring-Pass-Not section was very encouraging, as he explains how it acts as a force field that expands and protects you as you grow, and isn't just a barrier to hold you back. Fear, superstition, and ignorance disappear with this knowledge of our loving Grandfather Saturn's help.- Mel Tucker, Austin, TX

Robert's new book is a deep and thorough exploration of mighty Saturn, which he approaches with sage wisdom and his enlightened Uranian perspective. A unique and helpful treasure from the master astrologer.
– Michael Tyler, Chimacum, WA

In this work, Robert invites us to be friends with Saturn. It is indeed an original proposal and a high recommendation, since Saturn embodies the qualities to make us a Spiritual Master, which makes it a good friend to have. He offers that Saturn symbolizes the gateway to our true Self, and as we learn about it, we can understand ourselves. By its transits across our planets and through our houses and the conscious decisions we must make at each crucial point, we come to realize who and what we really are, where we are heading, why life is as it is, and how to take control of our life in an active way. Though I am not an astrologer, Robert's book is clear, synthetic, easy to read and understand, and well worth reading. - MN Ortiz Cué – Spain

CONTENTS

ACKNOWLEDGEMENTS...................................1

PREFACE..3

INTRODUCTION...7

CHAPTER 1 -
Making Friends with Saturn.........................11

CHAPTER 2 -
How Astrology Works................................ 29

CHAPTER 3 -
Who and What Is Saturn?............................65

CHAPTER 4 -
Saturn, Dharma, and Karma.........................87

CHAPTER 5 -
Saturn, Guardian Of The Ring-Pass-Not.............113

Part Two:
Saturn Transits - An Introduction.................. 133

CHAPTER 6 -
The Saturn Cycle - Conjunctions................... 135

CHAPTER 7 -
The Saturn Cycle - Squares And Oppositions.........155

CHAPTER 8 -
The Saturn Return...................................173

CHAPTER 9 -
The Progressed Moon, The Saturn Cycle,
and Critical Life Choices...................................189

CHAPTER 10 -
Saturn Conjunct Pluto for Everyone
on Earth 2003-2020......................................205

EPILOGUE -
Living The Spiritual Life...............................225

ABOUT THE AUTHOR.................................241

Acknowledgements

I would like to thank everyone involved in the process of creating this book, since any good work involves a community, each contributing something that makes the sum greater than the total of the parts. That's why my first thanks goes out to my on-line community, who have given me excellent feedback about my Saturn articles over the years and offered many suggestions for related topics, which gave my imagination something to contemplate.

I also want to acknowledge my appreciation for all who have been my readers at various points in the creative process. Each of you contributed one or more valuable insights pointing me in directions I may not have considered otherwise, and made this book a better written work with each passing month. All of you have my sincere gratitude for your willingness to take the time to read the drafts and offer me your insights.

I want to offer my highest gratitude to the very generous donor who made the Fifth Ray Publishing operation a reality, enabling me to create this work freed of the usual publishing and editorial politics. And finally, utmost appreciation goes out to Bernadette, my Associate Editor who brought her educator's eye to the work. Her patience and brilliant Mercury retrograde skills as a proofreader and language arts specialist found countless things I needed to fix or re-write to make this the extraordinary work I believe it to be.

Finally, I want to acknowledge the power of my own Saturn in giving me the experiences I needed to write about the subject with authenticity, and the persistence to keep writing even when the enormity of the task was overwhelming and impossibly time-consuming. I could never have written this work before my second Saturn return, and in writing this work at this time in my life, I was opened to a new view of how our inner Saturn works its patient understanding across time and experience, both in my life and the lives of countless clients and loved ones.

So here's to the Ancient of Days, the Wise Old Friend who guides us from ignorance to awareness and from fear to the wisdom of our Highest Self that never deserts us.

-Robert Wilkinson

PREFACE

What you are about to read was never intended to be a book. Because I had written several dozen articles on Saturn-related subjects, I thought it would be good to create a collection of those pieces, compose a little more, and offer it to students and practitioners of astrology.

I quickly found that was not going to happen, since each article required fleshing out a lot of concepts, and I found I had repeated themes across several pieces. I realized as separate articles the work didn't hang together the way I wanted. Rather than offer readers a bunch of disconnected and sometimes repetitive material about Saturn, I went ahead and jumped feet first into creating the work you are about to read. And yes, being about Saturn, it has truly been a Saturnian journey the entire way, taking a lot more time and energy than I originally thought, along with a tremendous precision in editing the material so what is written says exactly what I am trying to communicate.

As I assembled the material, I realized all of the topics fit into one of two parts; one part was the conceptual material about the nature of Saturn, both in our inner nature as well as external associations, whereas the other part was material about Saturn transits and how they relate to other natal and progressed factors in our charts, as well as a very important recent event affecting everyone in the world for many years to come.

In selecting the focus of the book, I wanted to create a work for both amateur and professional astrologers, as well as laypeople with an interest in self-improvement who may have little or no knowledge of astrology. I realized I had to find a way to offer the material so it was easy to read, understand, and use, and universal in its applicability.

That meant the work could not be a "standard astrology" text about Saturn, discussing potential meanings of Saturn in the signs and houses. There are already countless books offering those things, but they are of limited use to most people without a foundation in astrology. I also didn't want to get into Saturn aspects with the planets, since that is another work already in progress.

I chose instead to focus on the psycho-spiritual factors symbolized by Saturn in each of us, since in my life and experience, once we learn about this incredible power within us, we take command of our lives and responses in ways which will never desert us. To my knowledge, there aren't many texts exploring Saturn's association with the power within us to attain forms of worldly and spiritual mastery as a function of time and maturity.

There are times in this book when I introduced concepts but chose not to give specific examples of how they might manifest. That's because I want you, the reader, to see how they could apply in your own lives, based in your experience. I don't want to limit your imagination as to how certain traits, lessons, and challenges could have manifested, nor the ways you took command over situations which allowed you to come out of perceived powerlessness or victimization.

All the information in this book comes from my own direct experience and the realizations and concepts I've observed over my 45 years practicing astrology. While some subjects offered here are found in other forms in other texts, I am sure this is the only work offering this material in this particular way. Throughout the book you will find a unique blend of established astrological concepts, as well as psychological and spiritual concepts, related to the Saturn function within all of us.

There are some universals in the human experience. In this work we explore these in the context of our inner Saturn, and how we may best refine and perfect that inner function to achieve a more fulfilled life. As we understand our inner Saturn, we can chart our own course with a sense of purpose and power, fully living our lives in the highest, best way possible in alignment with our Higher Self.

* * * * * * * * *

We live on the cutting edge of historical changes unlike anything faced in recorded history. While much in our world seems "out of control" right now, those feelings really have more to do with the collective atmosphere than our individual karmas. We're all learning to navigate the subtle pulls in this "time out of time," and be more conscious in our responses to the life we're all experiencing simultaneously. The intensification of elements going on right now is pushing energy into a future we are creating, individually and collectively, as we focus and embrace a greater potential. Our challenge is to reject fear and confusion as inadequate and useless responses to our historical imperative of bringing forth the living seeds of the next Great Age of Aquarius.

We're moving into a long term era unknown for many thousands of years, and are the midwives and midhusbands of the advent of what in the Vedas has been termed the Dwapara Yuga, or the Age of Electromagnetic Remembrance. This transitional era has introduced all of us to a radically different sense of time, partially because in the coming era, we shall all be more aware of the fluidity of the concepts of space, time, self, energy, matter, and the process of evolution itself. We are moving into an awareness of subtle fields of energy which will forever destroy the illusion of separateness, and coming to an experience of the Oneness of all of life, both visible and invisible. Enjoy the moment, since events will continue to accelerate throughout the 21st century, challenging all of us to become fearless as we navigate the entry into a new long term era.

We are part of "All-That-Is." We are never separate from the One Life into which we are born, live, and die. We are Soul/Spirits who inhabit a collection of physical, emotional, and mental constructs making up our personality. We are Eternals. We learn to manage a body, a wide variety of both conflicted and harmonious feelings - the former learned, the latter your true Self - and a wide pallet of ideas, some more helpful than others. It's all part of being human!

The birth chart is the blueprint for our individual Matrix of Existence. It reveals the patterns we are born with, as well as those we are to develop. Our chart is the map plotting the course of how high we can aspire to go and how deep we will have to journey, through pleasurable and painful events and relationships, so we may become as humanly enlightened as we can be. Even though we are seemingly limited by circumstances, and wonder why things are the way they are, we always have the ability to be better and more effective at whatever we decide to do, or believe we could do.

As you read this work and contemplate various facets of life and your humanity, you may catch glimpses of entirely different ways to be fully human and fully Divine. There is a way beyond suffering. While no one can end another Being's suffering, as we choose to welcome the Way of Spiritual Mastery perfect for us, we can BE who we already are, freed from fear and suffering. This is the goal for all of us.

While I can't say I've perfectly found the Way, I know there is a path that once embraced, makes us greater human Soul/Spirits than we could ever imagine when we were lost in ignorance of our true Divine nature. This work may help you catch glimpses of your Way to becoming the embodiment of Goodness, Truth, Beauty, Compassion, and Understanding as you learn to live the Love, Wisdom, and Intelligent Action you are, always have been, and always will be. If even one door is opened, and a greater Way, Truth, and Life are glimpsed, then this work will have served its purpose.

INTRODUCTION
YOU ARE YOUR PLANETS

Astrology is the mathematical art and science of the cycles of life. Using astrology, we can correlate time with all that manifests in the material, emotional, mental, and spiritual levels of existence. It reveals the larger patterns of meaning at any given stage of life or experience, and because it measures cycles, astrology marks the "action beats" of how and when things appear and disappear, both in an individual life, as well as in the world at large.

Our life cycles begin at the first breath, and continue until the last. We have many cycles affecting us, some short, some long. Through the cycles of astrology, we can mark the stages of when anything begins, how it develops throughout its phases of manifestation, and how it ultimately fulfills itself at the appointed season. Through astrology, we can understand how any given thing came to be, and see the current and future "pulses" marking the major turning points in the life of that thing.

While the larger patterns in the cosmos reveal the tendencies and periods of significance in the world at large, they also gave each of us a unique cosmic pattern at the moment we were born. There is no other who has our exact birth chart. It is our "fingerprint in time." Each birth chart is one of a kind, and symbolizes an individual's path to their greatest potential and purpose for being alive on Earth.

The birth chart reveals our unique inner makeup, revealing facets of our Eternal Self as it was ex-pressed (literally "pressed out") into form at birth. It shows our

7

♄ Saturn: Spiritual Master, Spiritual Friend

specialized nature relative to the eternity we call time. It is our energy field, and at least for this lifetime, a unique energetic matrix of Being.

For those who accept reincarnation as a fact, each time we are born we are given a different hologram of our personalized electromagnetic field within the larger planetary and human field, showing us strengths and skills, as well as weaknesses and areas of growth. The eternal energy we ARE finds many ways to express itself as we learn what we must on the journey from darkness to Light.

Because the chart represents the energy field we "inhaled" at birth, it represents all factors within that field, as well as the evolving fields of life experiences as we grow and move in various environments. And since much of human experience works out through the people we encounter, besides representing inner character traits, the planets in a chart also represent significant people we meet along the path of life.

We and the universe do a dance throughout life, and while we often think external things drive activities and behavior, from another point of view, life is entirely conditioned by who we are, what we've learned, and how we are able to deal with the constantly changing conditions in life.

The birth chart indicates all of these things and more, because it is the picture of the frozen moment of our birth. The chart literally shows us the patterns of the cosmos at our first breath, the moment all of our life cycles are set into motion. The birth chart symbolizes our "nature" which will be "nurtured" many ways throughout life as we navigate both difficult and harmonious circumstances.

The planets are our "Lights," each related to various departments of life and personality traits. They express through the filters of the signs, and through their expression we come to know how best to respond to events given the strengths and weaknesses we are aware of. Birth planets symbolize inherent and evolved traits. As the planets move in their orbits throughout our lives, the traits associated with each also move in a dance of co-

♄ Saturn: Spiritual Master, Spiritual Friend

relation rather than causality.

Through this dance we actualize various potentials, fulfilling some patterns and generating others. The chart holds the secret to the timing in our lives, and the characteristics being created, built, challenged, stabilized, fulfilled, and ultimately dissolved, creating space for other traits to come forth.

While planets are external things, in the context of our birth chart they represent facets of who we ARE. From one angle of approach, we are our Sun. We are our enlightenment. We can't be any other enlightenment than who we are. We may find enlightenment through many routes, people, and ideas, and can always expand the forms of enlightenment we understand, but ultimately we will still be the Light we are, regardless of all external factors.

We are our Moon. We are our Mercury. We are our Venus, Mars, and Jupiter. And yes, we ARE our Saturn. It is not a force external to us. We entirely shape its response in our life, since we and our Saturn are One together. We will discuss more about this throughout this work.

Saturn represents the steel framework of the structure of the skyscraper of our lives. Saturn teaches us the limits of our Soul expression on Earth in any given life chapter, but they are not fixed limits. They are merely the temporary boundaries of various forms of self-expression originating in the family and cultural matrix we internalized when much younger. They provide us a reference as we honor those things which are true, good, and beautiful while transcending the limitations of self-expression preventing us from becoming spiritual adults.

In the final analysis, we are the ones who determine our "fate," and choose to move with the higher or the lower in every moment of life. As we embrace the journey of self-discovery, Saturn becomes our Spiritual Friend and Guide as we move through experiences teaching us when it's time to transcend old limitations because we have nothing left to learn from them.

9

♄ Saturn: Spiritual Master, Spiritual Friend

We are never controlled or limited by the birth chart, since we and our chart are one. It is an abstract for our entry into this world. While it shows us the larger patterns of existence, it does not deny us anything we need to learn or experience. The only thing limiting us is our ability or inability to respond to the challenges of life on Earth as an Eternal having a human experience.

However, while we are not limited by the chart, it could be said we never exactly transcend it. We cannot be other than who we are. And yet that changes ten thousand ways as we live life, and come to new realizations about who we are and who we aren't as various life chapters unfold. While we never transcend who we are, as we live our eternal Quest, we become greater than we imagined, adding more and more facets to the ever evolving jewel of our evolving Higher Self.

So let's begin the journey of discovering what this thing called Saturn is all about, and along the way, hopefully we will catch glimpses of how to embrace our greater destiny and leave behind confused ways of living and responding to the potential of becoming more than we have ever imagined.

10

♄ Saturn: Spiritual Master, Spiritual Friend

CHAPTER 1
MAKING FRIENDS WITH SATURN

Most people really don't like Saturn. Saturn is associated with all that holds us down, or makes us afraid, and those times in life when we must do something we really don't want to do. Saturn doesn't seem to cut us much slack, and when it's active, we often feel stuck, limited, or held back.

Saturn will seem to be the worst enemy you will ever know, until you make that inner power your friend. Through Saturn, we learn to face fear, frustration, and feelings of being trapped, chained, or weighted down by seemingly unbearable limitations. Yet through it all, no matter how oppressed we feel, Saturn beckons us to recognize and welcome the sense of purpose it holds for us so we can throw off the chains of mental slavery, and claim our part to play as a mature spiritual Being.

Just how do we "make friends with Saturn?" That seems to be one of the hardest things we'll ever do, given Saturn's relentlessly unyielding qualities. Those who have studied astrology often are told Saturn makes life hard, and is associated with continual burdens. I even once read nothing good comes from Saturn. Since this is not true, let's take a look at the virtues associated with Saturn, and examine ways to make friends with those energies so they work for good in our lives.

♄ Saturn: Spiritual Master, Spiritual Friend

WHAT IS SATURN?

I suppose we should start with exploring Saturn's qualities in order to know it better. In traditional astrology, it is associated with aging, fear, control, restraint, duty, obligations, and limitations. However, Saturn is also the part of us which is responsible and willing to learn those things we have to learn, doing what we know we have to do, even when it's unpleasant or difficult. Saturn shows us how we become mature, and teaches us patience, persistence, determination, organization, and wisdom in dealing with things we'd rather not deal with.

It may be helpful to imagine Saturn as "the Old Wise Friend," an inner "Ancient of Days," who presents us mortals with opportunities to practice the virtues of thorough self-discipline, organized approaches, and consistent effort so we may learn to recognize, trust, and have self-confidence in what we have achieved. If we're open, this "severe elder" over time will show us a warm and wise heart and a clearer sense of purpose as it guides us on the path to Higher Awareness. While Saturn can be a stern disciplinarian, as we accept this profound inner power, we will find it to be the oldest, wisest friend we've ever known, helping guide us along our orbit around the Sun, symbolizing our Light and Life.

Saturn is the great humbler. Saturn shows us where our cultural biases and limitations meet our transpersonal obligations and the Higher Law of our Being. It's where our worldly rubber meets the spiritual road. And when our karma runs over our dogma enough times, we learn humility and open to greater possibilities if we can find the right point of view about those lessons.

Saturn, besides representing our attitude as we approach and deal with the responsibilities in life, demonstrates the limits of our "response-ability." It is the measure of our ability to respond to the requirements of the moment. How we choose to respond to circumstances is said to be the one power we have that allows us to

12

♄ Saturn: Spiritual Master, Spiritual Friend

overcome adversity and move into more fulfilling actions, feelings, and thoughts.

This inner power teaches us how to recognize and work within reasonable limitations to become clear about how we can consciously create or deal with real world situations. Through Saturn we learn what we can and cannot control or even affect, given the limiting conditions in circumstances we may or may not have had a part in creating. Regardless of our part (or no part) in creating the hectic situations we confront from time to time, we still have to learn to manage our personality and do the best we can within those conditions.

Saturn represents the power within us which compels growth over time, becoming more aware (and "realistic," for better or worse) as a result of life experiences. It is said Jupiter brings us the lessons we may or may not learn, whereas Saturn brings us the lessons we *must* learn. We can embrace these necessary lessons, or reject them, or like them, or not like them, but we will go through them regardless of what we think or feel. Saturn reveals our willingness to grow into a greater maturity and do our part in the right way and time as we navigate the way from limited to greater understanding and awareness.

And yes, Saturn is associated with those things we fear and why we fear them. It is how and why we become burdened by heaviness, depression, anxiety, apprehension, bitterness, pessimism, taking things too seriously in negative ways, or a sense of struggling with being bound by conditions over which we have little or no control. How much we struggle with them indicates how much work it will take to make Saturn our friend. When we would rather argue our limitations than find a solution to a problem, it is clearly a time when we are confronting a challenge and need to make Saturn our friend.

It's easy to be at peace with Saturn, once we know the qualities it represents in our inner nature, and how it conditions elements of the evolutionary process which

♄ Saturn: Spiritual Master, Spiritual Friend

shape our personality. Saturn is said to "rule time," and many of its keywords involve learning how to use time to best effect. When we totally adopt Saturn's virtues, we are truly living the path to mastery since there is no separation between our inner Saturn function and how we demonstrate our "ability to respond."

Since Saturn is said to rule time and the binding force of time, it's probably best not to be in too much of a hurry as we learn how to craft a friendship with Saturn! Let's begin with Saturn's duality, and how Saturn makes our path to self-mastery crystal clear.

SATURN - MASTERY OR SLAVERY

All the Seven Sacred Planets in astrology (those that are visible) have a duality in how they express their qualities in our lives, for better and for worse. Each has a healthy or functional expression, as well as an unhealthy, or dysfunctional expression. We will explore all the planetary dualities in Chapter Two.

Saturn's duality is Dominion vs Slavery, and represents how we deal with limitation and whether we are limiting others or being limited by others in healthy or unhealthy ways. As we become more aware of how Saturn functions in our inner and outer life, and transmute negative tendencies into positive, effective responses, we come out of being "slavers or enslaved." Once we have made Saturn our friend, we no longer have to learn not to control or be oppressed by being controlled, since we're charting our own course.

Saturn shows us the way to become the conscious authors of our own existence. Through negative Saturn experiences we are challenged to come to a consistent patience and mature understanding of what we do and do not have to put up with. As we learn how to let go of inappropriate things and are willing to accept what we must dare, do, and know, we can find facets of our purpose for

♄ Saturn: Spiritual Master, Spiritual Friend

being here and the means to express the wisdom we have gained from life experience.

Saturn is how we come to know the limits of our ability to influence things and people, and understand how to grow in effectiveness. As our understanding matures, we can become focused, purposeful, and wise as we consciously participate in the "Great Work," proactively accepting higher responsibilities in ever more effective forms of practical service that can benefit the world.

As noted earlier, when we are burdened by heaviness, depression, dread, being bound by conditions, or any of those other states where we feel trapped by chains of mental slavery, it *always* indicates a time when we are learning about Saturn. By learning how to respond in mature and mindful ways when the burden is heavy, we make Saturn our friend, time our ally, and calculated patience the means by which we come out of being bound by obsolete rules, structures, and unnecessary limits.

Cultivating Saturn's strengths allows us to overcome any tendency to get caught in negative thoughts and feelings when navigating life changes so negativity doesn't hinder us in the future. A great benefit is that we find over time the understanding we've gained and the methods we've learned serve us to help others who are experiencing similar negative mental and emotional states so they can get clear about how they can transform their negative Saturn responses as well.

Because we evolve and life goes on with different lessons appropriate to each new life chapter we live, from time to time we are required to take a hard look at the structure and assumptions of our life narrative, and how negative Saturn traits and ineffective responses came to be lodged in our minds and attitudes. By knowing the cause of those negative Saturn responses and expressions, we can eliminate many of them at the root.

Life's difficulties result from the mind getting stuck in patterns which generate suffering rather than happiness and fulfillment. When Saturn is our friend, through

15

ℏ Saturn: Spiritual Master, Spiritual Friend

knowing we have the ability to change our response to outer circumstances, we can come out of feeling trapped by conditions. While it may take time, as we practice Saturn's virtues we eventually attain mastery over ourselves, and therefore over Life.

ENDING SUFFERING - GENERATING WISDOM

We are told by ancient sources there are four things that generate suffering; attachments, aversions, illusions, and the mind suffering over its own suffering, often expressed via the mind's natural pessimism. These are the root of most human problems. However, since we are Eternals having human experiences, we're not here to stay stuck in suffering. Much of life involves learning how to break the link between pain and suffering. While life can be painful, we do not have to suffer. This theme will be explored throughout this book.

It takes Saturn's discipline, determination, consistency, structure, and "command and control" functions to practice the antidotes for suffering in a consistent organized way. Saturn brings us understanding when we must detach, whether from suffering over difficulty or apprehension that the good we've found will end. If life is a time stream in an ever-changing set of conditions, then any attachment to having things "stay the same" is an exercise in futility.

Through Saturn we come to know when it's time to take a dispassionate look at circumstances or people and find an objective view of those things we do and do not need to be involved with. Our inner Saturn teaches us to face things exactly as they are, without fearing what we're seeing, or might see. We need Saturn's self-organizing pursuit of an integrated experiential wisdom to find the practical Divine discrimination to know what is truly real, what is conditionally real, what is apparently real, and what is unreal. And we need Saturn's patience to bring the

16

Saturn: Spiritual Master, Spiritual Friend

mind's pessimism under control so we may use Saturn's discipline to steer our mind into more productive directions as we need to. Saturn helps us restructure unhelpful mental patterns so we can find clarity and understanding as we move through difficult feelings, whether they originated in the past, or are coming up due to present issues.

We come to understanding and wisdom through life experiences. While some of them seem to be unique unto themselves, other times we encounter people, things, and circumstances which remind us of past difficulties, challenges, defeats, and triumphs. Of course, we may or may not be consciously aware we're emotionally reacting to something from the past. Many times we have old response patterns residing in the subconscious mind and we're not even aware of how they're impacting our sense of competency, self-esteem, or how they may be shaping or limiting our self-expression during challenging experiences.

Whether we're conscious of the forces shaping our responses or not, time and experience work together through our Saturn function to bring us to critical life junctures where we get opportunities to choose to resolve past experiences through changing old responses, and find new understanding and wisdom. These crucial points of choice are associated with the cycles of our progressed Moon as it dances with transiting Saturn.

The interaction between the progressed Moon and transiting Saturn represents an interactive dynamic marking regular life intervals when we re-feel the process of our life and evolution as we've grown from birth to where we're at right now. The progressed Moon absorbs life experience as it transits through all the signs every 27+ years. Transiting Saturn brings us the "hard lessons" in the outer world after the feeling impressions we absorb through the progressed Moon. In Chapter Nine we'll take an in-depth look at the dance between the progressed Moon and transiting Saturn, and the major changes we confront at points throughout life.

♄ Saturn: Spiritual Master, Spiritual Friend

Naturally, there are other progressions and transits besides these two specific cycles which bring experiences with people and circumstances that may trigger old memories and unresolved internal issues. Significant planetary transits often bring important reminders of past events and echoes of past experiences, depending on the planetary quality. To a greater or lesser degree, all transits and progressions bring up echoes of memories of patterns from the past showing us how much they influenced our subconscious mind and subsequent responses. The evolution of our perception is a continuum, so from one angle, we can track anything we confront at any point in life to its time source, and learn which patterns need transmuting.

All life experiences serve to bring us out of ignorance into greater awareness. All of them reveal our power to choose how we want to act with intention to express our evolving mastery over life. Many roads lead us home.

Regardless of which life experiences trigger unresolved issues and why, it could be said through Saturn we find the only thing that really matters is how we respond to difficult feelings and experiences. Most feelings of inadequacy, fear, and other unhelpful emotional states have their roots in the past. Breaking free of counterproductive emotions requires a structured self-disciplined care plan. Our inner Saturn assists us in crafting an organized care plan perfect for our evolution in each chapter of life.

Making Saturn our friend gives us opportunities over time to heal wounds associated with unresolved issues creating difficulty. Saturn allows us to restructure our responses, appropriate to healing conflicted internal states of thinking and feeling. Saturn demonstrates how we must take responsibility for doing what needs to be done to step outside of limitations and fear we no longer need to live with.

HEALING CHILDHOOD WOUNDS

We were all born into a family living within a cultural matrix. We came into this existence enveloped by certain interpersonal and transpersonal set of values and circumstances we did not create, even if we did choose to be born within those specific matrix conditions and situations. These determined the field of our initial experience from which we branched out. We'll go into the family and cultural matrix and how it conditions our views and responses in Chapter Four where we examine how Karma and Dharma influence our lives.

Most of us had a childhood with mixed experiences. Some were healthy and nurtured the positive in us. This is why we feel confident in some life areas. However, other experiences wounded us, and hurt us deeply.

At least one of our wounds was an archetypal "Sacred Wound," binding us to all others who share these wounds across space and time. This is covered in great depth in Chapter Four in the section exploring the difference between what I have termed "Big K Karma" and "little k karma." There is a huge difference in the wounds associated with each.

While some life wounds occurred due to another's ignorance and/or fear playing out in our lives, other wounds were the result of our ignorance or obedience to ideas and attitudes we assumed were true. Ultimately, whether a wound was generated by our own or another's behavior, all wounds challenge us to grow beyond ego limitations, and become the expression of our Higher Self.

Most of us were wounded in childhood as a result of karma and the free will of others who may or may not have been conscious of how they were hurting the people in their lives. Because we were young and vulnerable, when we went through primal woundings, it created negative responses which may still reside in the subconscious mind. These are the source of the anxiety that arises when we think of going back into those old

♄ Saturn: Spiritual Master, Spiritual Friend

feelings and experiences.

However, if we are to throw off the mental and emotional chains hindering our ability to lead a fulfilling life, we must accept we have the power to overcome all we fear. Although negative early life experiences can be challenging, we find liberation as we learn not to clutch at the dread and shame linked to those memories.

When Saturn is our friend, we have the ultimate Wise One as a guide and counsel. Then we don't have to be afraid of anything or react to distressing experiences from a state of panic or avoidance. Mastering how we respond to life's experiences is the way to spiritual maturity. Saturn moves us from the theoretical to the actual, and shows us how well we've mastered the understanding and skills we need at each turn of the wheel of life.

In fact, as we welcome the Great Work and come into true spiritual maturity, we learn not to be afraid, and find love, wisdom, courage, and compassion when we are re-experiencing the toughest parts of our life story. Saturn's quality of spiritual maturity allows us to "return to the scene of the crime" and take charge of our responses rather than stay stuck feeling badly or inadequate. Over time and experience we no longer feel fear or anxiety related to past events, and we are free to be our Higher Self in ways more appropriate to the life chapter we're in.

Because of our resonance with other Soul/Spirits on the eternal planes of existence, we are born into families that show us how we are to learn to live, both similarly and differently from those family systems and values. All families nurture, but what needs to be nurtured means different things to different families. Are the patterns healthy or harmful? (I've found they're usually some of both!) Are they liberating or enslaving? Again, often there are a bit of both in any family.

Still, we are not bound to family patterns, even if the Great Work requires us to learn how to be loving to family members, whether they reciprocate or not. Though there is much that is not likable in this world, our task is to

♄ Saturn: Spiritual Master, Spiritual Friend

become the living expression of unconditional Love. This usually means we have to go through experiences requiring radical detachment from non-loving responses.

Though we may have had a difficult early family life, we don't have to live in self-pitying victim states. While it's natural for our mental "scratchy grooves" to get stuck in "why didn't they"..."how could they"... "couldn't they see" and other frictional thoughts, when Saturn is our friend we understand it's okay to be disappointed if it leads us to self-nurture, a healthy sense of boundaries, and a clear sense of the value of the limits of loyalty and disinterestedness. When we decide to nourish ourselves according to our need, and not accept crushed stone from another, it begins a whole new life and opens a whole new world.

While many things can trigger a memory of old experiences, in every case we can come out of heaviness by remembering we are spiritual adults and Eternals. We all have a Divine heritage allowing us to take command of our physical, emotional, and mental vehicles and how we experience our miraculous uniqueness in space-time. Saturn allows us to choose a wiser, more mature self-expression and forever leave behind feeling trapped in the "wounded child" state of consciousness.

When we re-experience echoes of childhood traumas, Saturn reminds us how we have matured and why we do not have to experience life as we did when we were a child. Through maturity and experience we can choose not to suffer or remain in the wounded child state of learned helplessness. By sheer evolutionary necessity, as we embrace Saturn's guidance throughout life, we learn to position our view in mature ways that empower us to live the wisdom of the truths we've found on our life journey from insecurity to power.

LETTING GO, SAYING GOOD-BYE

The natural innocence we were born with gets clothed in personality traits which evolve over time, offering us ways to adapt to ever-changing circumstances. All the changes we go through must occur because we need to individualize as a function of the evolutionary process. These force us to shift the direction and focus of how we do what we do in life areas needing attention. When it's time to focus our life trajectory in new directions, it usually means saying goodbye to old ways as newer, more important life experiences occur.

It is very human to become attached to familiar ways of doing our Being, and familiar faces we meet along the way. However, because life involves leaving behind many things, ideas, and people as we age, it is natural to feel a twinge of sadness when one chapter ends and another begins, and grieve those things we have lost, if only for a short while.

Sadness and grief are a natural part of the human condition. They show us the way to a greater, deeper, and wider love, once we get over judgments about whether we're grieving the right way, or conforming to the standards which "consensus reality" seeks to impose on our evolving perspective. And we must evolve when it's time to say good-bye.

However, while sadness and grief are universals for all of us, unfortunately they are often mistaken for "depression." A true depression means something is being forced down that needs to come up. Open displays of grief are not a "depression." They are a natural organic way to express genuine feelings related to loss. While life is indeed heavy at times - usually associated with Saturn transits and/or progressions! - these mark points in evolution where we must throw off our chains and take responsibility for restructuring how we express our Higher Self the best we're able.

Difficult times that feel heavy challenge us to find

♄ Saturn: Spiritual Master, Spiritual Friend

ways to take care of ourselves even when we feel weak or inadequate. When we are under heavy pressure, being patient, thoughtful, disciplined, mature, wise, and all the other positive Saturn qualities will antidote any emotional or mental patterns leading to pessimism, weakness, depression, repression, defeatism, and other negative states of mind.

It is always helpful to remember negative states of thinking and feeling are fundamentally unreal due to their impermanence. In other words, they will pass if we don't feed them, clutch at them, or give them any more power than they deserve, which is none at all.

Throughout life we learn to accept that our truth, our feelings, and how we choose to "do our Being" are okay even when no one in our family (or anyone else) validated them, or do not approve of them now. Saturn may accompany months or years of pain as we shed an ocean of tears when feeling isolated, alone and misunderstood, but as we willingly embrace our inner Saturn we become a more understanding and compassionate person. Saturn allows us to stand secure in our sense of purpose, free from fear of others' disapproval.

If we're willing to walk the walk, learning all we must learn, then joy comes after the sadness is spent, along with a new light and life. Saturn helps us take the time to understand and care for those things we believe are important. This creates the ability to know what really matters in any given experience.

As we learn what's important and how to care for those things which truly matter to us, we naturally encounter others who are learning how to care for themselves and what matters to them. Over time instead of asking for love, or feeling unloved, we learn how to love and be loving according to the dictates of our Higher Self. That's when we are attuned to the heart of Nature Herself, where we will find a healing lasting beyond time.

♄ Saturn: Spiritual Master, Spiritual Friend

CHANGING PATTERNS, TAKING POWER

All of Nature is a complex and infinite series of patterns. As our scope of understanding expands regarding how life lessons relate to personality growth and what we are to do in the world, we can discern elements of why we're here. The various patterns in our lives give us clues whereby we can come into a larger perspective about things, resources, the players and their roles, and our own relationship to expectations.

A good deal of human life is about navigating the ups and downs as we go around and around in patterns of recurring experience. As we learn to see the recurring elements and issues in life, we can choose what we want to change and how to replace old patterns with more fulfilling responses.

By knowing the patterns to keep and the patterns to change, all of us, you and me and humanity, are being led beyond old roles and limitations associated with narrower states of Being. Since each of us is a seed within the greater Life of humanity as a whole, each lesson we master aids the progress of all.

Over time, as we update how we view the way certain patterns have shaped our lives and responses, we can restructure those which no longer fulfill our sense of purpose or effectiveness. By examining how and why we are bound to certain patterns of acting, both those that are voluntary and those that are involuntary, we can break free of obsolete or deadening ways of living, and move into our place in the larger scheme of the Eternal Life, fully living our purpose for being alive.

As we change our patterns, we change how we experience our current existence, and we change the experiences we'll confront in the future. As we change how and what we experience, everything becomes grist for the mill of Soul. Eventually, we don't suffer as we once did, and are able to maintain a calm equipoise even in the midst of the worst inner or outer storms.

24

ℏ Saturn: Spiritual Master, Spiritual Friend

Over the long run, this helps us stay focused on the things we believe are real rather than unreal, and identify with our Higher Self instead of the frustrations of the lower self. The mind and feelings are inherently restless, and usually lack discipline. That's why we need to cultivate the power to reference the higher rather than identify with the lower.

We always have that ability in the here and now, but it must be practiced regularly in an organized, disciplined way if we want to create consistently productive responses. This is why it's not helpful to go into judgments and comparisons with the experiences others are going through, or how well they seem to be dealing with their hard lessons. Each has their own lessons to learn in their own way, and as a result of what we have learned, we can help others, and be helped by others.

Life can be painful for all kinds of reasons, but we do not have to suffer one instant longer than necessary. Even when we feel hopelessness, defeatism, discouragement, fatigue, and all the other attributes of the mind suffering over its own suffering, we can still instantly choose to change our response patterns and redirect our minds to better things.

Welcome to the school all of us are subjected to, by nature of life in a three dimensional form in an impermanent world! Begin to frame everything which presents itself to you with an eye to opening your heart to an ever-greater group recognition, effective service, and self-forgetfulness, coupled to an ever-greater expression of goodwill. Eventually your expressions of Love will become more consistent, you'll know your connectedness with other beings, and you'll drop all of your fears very quickly.

By generating goodwill and positivity, you're using spiritual magnetic material in a loving and wise way. As you practice this Divine awareness, all limitations of form can be seen in the light of a more mature spiritual understanding, with all things redeemed in good fashion. Then your imagination becomes the defining limit of your spirituality in your world, according to the level of your

ħ Saturn: Spiritual Master, Spiritual Friend

effectiveness and the specific function you are occupying within the Loving Light we all are together.

Though much of this sounds difficult to achieve, it's really an inevitability once you get in the groove and stay on track through time and experience. Keep synthesizing your awareness as you move from realization to application to further realizations and applications. The fantastic goal of perfecting our consciousness through practices of self-realization is within reach for us all, if we simply come to the right point of view and show up, ready to play!

As we make ourselves the embodiment and expression of a "friendly" Saturn, we come into an ever more effective understanding of the limits and possibilities in any given moment or situation. Then we are no longer at the mercy of external events. Over time, practicing Saturn's virtues and positive qualities leads us to the understanding, wisdom, and skills demonstrating how far we have come on our Higher Path to becoming Masters of the Wisdom.

As we walk this Higher Way, we find instead of needing help, we become helpers. Instead of seeking compassion, we become the embodiment of compassion. One of the great values of compassion, or "fellow feeling," is its power to antidote any tendency to suffer in the midst of difficult conditions, which allows many negative states of mind to be washed into the ocean of Divine Forgiveness.

* * * * * * * * *

Now that we've begun exploring a bit about the importance of Saturn on our journey through life, it's time to take a look at the fundamentals of astrology and how it works. This will provide a context for Saturn's all-important place and function in the cosmic choir of the planetary "Lights" and give you an overview of how everything fits together in the remarkable art and science we call

♄ Saturn: Spiritual Master, Spiritual Friend

astrology. In Chapter Three, we'll pick back up with more about our inner Saturn, its qualities, what it teaches us, how to take command of our destiny, and how to make the most of this "Spiritual Master, Spiritual Friend."

♄ Saturn: Spiritual Master, Spiritual Friend

CHAPTER 2

HOW ASTROLOGY WORKS

♈ ♉ ♊ ♋ ♌ ♍ ♎ ♏ ♐ ♑ ♒ ♓

For readers who are not familiar with Saturn and the dynamics of astrology, this chapter will provide some fundamental information about various basic and essential elements in astrology and their meaning. While this won't be exhaustive, it will be valuable in explaining how the symbols of astrology define the components of personality and life, as well as how transits and timing help us take command of "the Great Work" of refining and integrating our conscious intention to become the highest, best Self we can be.

Before we begin this exploration of basic astrology, I want to make one essential thing very clear: the planets do *not* make anything happen. We alone create our lives through the consequences of our actions and inactions and how we choose to respond. As the Bard of Avon famously wrote, "The fault, dear Brutus, lies not in our stars, but in ourselves if we are underlings."

Astrology's dictum for many thousands of years, "As Above So Below," points us to the fact there is a non-causal correspondence between celestial and Earthly patterns. By understanding the correspondences between "the above and the below" in our lives, we can see more clearly the limits of our responsibility for the causes set into motion and effects we experience throughout this life.

Life patterns and karmas play out through the choices we make to act or not act. Through these we learn

♄ Saturn: Spiritual Master, Spiritual Friend

Divine discrimination. It is through our actions or non-actions, and whether these are in our best interests and can really get our intention accomplished, that we determine what happens in life. The stars, whether natal, progressed, transits, or return charts done for specific places, cannot make anything happen of themselves. Nor can any astrological, Tarot, psychic, or "spiritual" self-help reading make a thing happen or not happen.

Regardless of our use astrology or some other form of guidance, in the final analysis we live our lives and make choices. We are the ones who are acting, reacting, or being acted upon. While the planetary qualities and aspects indicate what is favorable or unfavorable for us to do, they do not compel some good or bad event to happen.

The birth chart shows our natural qualities and the timing on when we will confront choices and changes, but not how we will respond to them. An astrological configuration cannot make us act appropriately, or solve a problem in and of itself. Many types of configurations occur as we live our lives, with "good ones" not magically bringing expected good, nor "bad ones" visiting disaster upon us.

Any personal configuration only manifests to the degree we are living life, and not merely being spectators waiting for something to happen. Of course there are configurations associated with changes affecting large groups of people and global events, but even in these cases, we still must find the right ways to act or not act.

We are not "ruled by the stars," but we are a snapshot of the solar system at a certain point in space-time holding the mystery of why we chose to incarnate then. The chart reveals the material, emotional, mental, and spiritual tendencies to be worked out on the personal, interpersonal, and transpersonal levels of life.

As we master these twelve "frequency zones of human existence," we become the living embodiment of Divine Love, Wisdom, and Intelligence in Action. From a spiritual angle, the chart is a picture of our fragmentedness

♄ Saturn: Spiritual Master, Spiritual Friend

and our wholeness, our uniqueness and what we share with all others across space and time.

The birth chart maps the play of various parts of our personality within the wholeness of existence. From one point of view, the chart is pure potential. No planet is good, no planet is bad; no sign or house position is good or bad, and no aspect is good or bad unto itself. Everything is related to everything else, and the infinite complexity of life guarantees what seems good at one time may be useless or counterproductive in another.

The chart marks the "time vintage" we are a part of, as well as our essential individuality. It holds the mystery of the parts of personality to be developed, and ultimately transcended. Above all, it is a time map of the life events that will shape us through the choices we'll make. In a sense, it's both a road atlas and a weather report, showing us the schedule of our appointments with destiny.

The birth chart is a unique blueprint of the "house of personality," our incarnated vehicle for the expression of our Soul/Spirit. It could be said the chart indicates various factors in our "essential nature." How this expresses itself in the world is conditioned by another all-important factor. Besides the "essential nature" indicated by the birth chart, we are also shaped by how our family and cultural matrix influence our responses, which in turn impacts what manifests and why we must go through certain experiences.

This is the "nurture" part of the human equation. We all are challenged to understand what does and does not nurture us. This changes as a function of growth and what we say "yes" to and say "no" to as we move through life experiences and create our lives and destinies. In a later chapter, we shall explore how much power the family and cultural matrix has over us until we learn consciously to choose which values and structures to hold on to at each turn of the wheel of life, and which ones we will leave behind.

FATE VS FREE WILL

There are only two things "fated" or "destined" for us humans. 1) to be born where we were, when we were, to the genetic makeup, heritage, and cultural matrix of our parents, and 2) the timing of certain choices. Not what choices we will make, but the necessity of choosing at specific points in space and time what we will or will not do. These points of choice and decision are built into our clock. All else is "free will."

While we may ultimately have the free will to choose our course at any given point in time, we usually find many options are limited when we are dealing with another person or in a collective situation. That's because they also have the free will to choose their responses to the experience we share. Then we can only choose for ourselves, even though we may want to choose something to benefit both of us, or benefit a greater collective circumstance.

In any area involving someone else's free will, things are not entirely under our control. We can only do the best we are able under those circumstances. In difficult situations, the trick is to remember to listen to the inner voice telling us what we need to do to move through and beyond the difficulty and into a better head and heart space.

Within the great dualistic field we live, we humans are given five senses and a mind to learn through changing conditions how to be fully "Divine" in our human-ness. This implies that beyond dualistic frames like "good and bad," "right and wrong," there is a place for forms of both harmonious and disharmonious experiences at points in evolution. All life experiences show us how to BE our highest aspiration of self-expression, and bring forth more refined and worthy fruits of our various labors in this world. When we understand the dualisms of existence, we have the power to overcome all forms of suffering, and find a joyous enthusiasm of living, knowing we are moving

♄ Saturn: Spiritual Master, Spiritual Friend

toward an integrated better future.

As we open to a greater understanding of the meaning of any experience, we find we have a wider range of possible productive responses to any situation. Over time we find we are no longer trapped by a lack of imagination, and can use conscious intention to shape our response to any situation that presents itself.

As times change, the demands on our lives and talents change. What once worked for us no longer does, or is no longer applicable to the present situation. Old skills no longer apply, old attitudes are out of place. These create dynamic conditions where we eventually must consciously choose whether we want to stay stuck in attachment, aversion, delusion, or pessimism enslaving our imagination, or whether we are willing to try new ways of living forms of Love, Wisdom, and Intelligence.

Astrology illustrates our freedom to choose how we will respond to circumstances we may or may not have had a part in creating. It simultaneously indicates the limitations inherent in the life situations we have to go through. At its best, astrology offers us optimum times to replace old unhelpful responses with actions, feelings, and thoughts allowing us to generate more positive experiences in the future.

The quicker we understand the antidotes for unfortunate behaviors, the quicker we can reorient toward something better than we had before. Sometimes, though, we must dismantle or even tear down old structures of doing and being to create space for our new self to manifest. This is where we learn the planetary qualities we need to use constructively, usually through seeing its dysfunctional side.

Any time you confront a dysfunctional part of you, another person, or a situation, your chart indicates which of the "planetary lights" needs to change manifestation. Each of the planets has two expressions, constructive and destructive. When functioning in a healthy way, the planets manifest as personality strengths giving us power to bring forth health, wealth, love, and perfect self-expression for

♄ Saturn: Spiritual Master, Spiritual Friend

ourselves and others. They bring forth positive events and conditions, or at the very least, allow us to navigate difficulty in ways that are perfect for us. When operating in a dysfunctional way, they bring maladjusted conditions, difficulties, and problems, usually through behaviors which create suffering for us and others. Those are the times when we are challenged to change how we express those planetary functions so they are in our highest interests.

Now let's take a look at the four key factors in astrology to understand how it works.

THE SEVEN SACRED PLANETS

There are four fundamental building blocks in astrology. They are the planets, signs, houses, and aspects. Everything else is commentary on these four primary factors.

Each of the planets represents a "Light" within us, and each is important in showing us our inner makeup, and how we are inclined to respond to circumstances. Each planet has its own "department of labor," or area of influence. So what are the departments assigned to the "Inner Lights?" astrology provides us a structure for the various energies of our personality.

We'll begin with the Sun, symbolizing the illumination principle. The Sun is the Light/Life we ARE. It is our power plant where we shine out an integral, integrated integrity. It is the center of our personal solar system and the giver of life.

The Sun's duality is **Fruitfulness/Sterility**. *This is the aspect of consciousness describing our making of growth or deserts in our life and the lives of others.* * By our Solar function we shine forth pride, inflexibility, sense

♄ Saturn: Spiritual Master, Spiritual Friend

of entitlement or inability to bless others, so we may come to know how to be the living light of purpose and integrity, bringing forth life and abundance for self and others.

The Moon symbolizes the reflective principle and way of feeling immediate experience. It is the sum of our habits and immediate feeling responses in the here and now. The Moon is the "shell of personality" continually shaped through imitation, reflection, and emotional receptivity as we move through life experiences.

The Moon's duality is **Peace/Strife.** *This is the aspect of consciousness describing how subconsciousness responds to the immediacy of our experience.** By our Lunar function we fall into dependency, clutching, or backward-looking insecurity, and thus come to know how to provide for the need of the moment in a mature and sensitive way, resting secure in our instinctive awareness while protecting what is valuable and nurturing what needs care.

Mercury represents how we process and coordinate ideas and details of all the things we have to do. It is how we integrate Spirit, Soul, and matter using "receptive mind." Mercury, also known as Hermes, is the Guide of Souls.

Mercury's duality is **Life/Death.** *This is the aspect of consciousness that can as easily create as destroy.** By our Mercury function we create chaos and disorganized scattered conditions through ambivalence and distractibility, and thus come to see how to adapt to ever newer information, allowing us to see a more effective order and priority of action, thought, and feeling. Mercury teaches us to use discernment as we coordinate various functions to bring forth perfect knowing of how to do whatever needs to be done in each particular situation.

Venus represents what we like and find beautiful, attractive, and valuable. It is associated with those things we idealize, and represents our cooperative, creative, and romantic inclinations. It symbolizes social emotions, and as its symbol is a hand mirror, it represents our vanities, charm, and aesthetic inclinations.

35

♄ Saturn: Spiritual Master, Spiritual Friend

Venus' duality is **Wisdom/Folly.** *This is the aspect of consciousness describing our subconscious response to self-consciousness, affecting our "mental offspring."* * By our Venus function we live our vanities, selfishness, or narcissistic ways of relating, so we may come to know how to capture more beautiful forms of an inner picture of a higher, refined, elegant life and relationships in the perfect ways, places, and times.

Mars represents how we mobilize, activate, and rise to immediate challenges. It is said to be the "fight or flight" principle and how we "attack the problems of life." Mars spurs us to action, and symbolizes the way we mobilize in the here and now, and how we advance and retreat while moving through our desires and interactions with people and circumstances.

Mars' duality is **Grace/Sin.** *This is the aspect of consciousness that shows whether our responses are manifesting error or truth, maladjustment or beauty.** By our Martian function we force things before their time or confront abrasive, aggressive, or hostile energies in ourselves and others, and thus we learn how to sever what must be severed, and further what must be furthered, quickly and directly. (As an aside, the original meaning of "sin" had nothing to do with moral failure. It was an archery term meaning "to miss the mark," or not hitting the center of a target. I use it here in that sense.)

Jupiter represents imagination, "optimistic mind," and how we see opportunity and truth. Jupiter's duality is **Wealth/Poverty.** *This is the aspect of consciousness showing how we are grasping circumstances with abundance or neediness.** By our Jupiterian function we waste time, energy, or money, or are expansive in ways others can mistake for weakness, and thus learn to use what we are given so our vision can be made real. This part of personality teaches us to understand the eternal abundance of the Universe by giving us those things we need when we need them. Saturn teaches us to accept them and use them wisely.

♄ Saturn: Spiritual Master, Spiritual Friend

This brings us to the roles Jupiter and Saturn together play in our lives. Jupiter is how we expand our vision and sense of what's possible. Jupiter is the cosmic therapist who gets us the psychological help we need when we need it, and frees us for new life adventures. Saturn represents the boundaries of our expansive experience, and how we are limited by necessity as well as fear. Whereas Jupiter wants to believe all things are possible, it also shows how we run away from those things we believe are too much trouble. Saturn reveals the path to taking command of our life and responses, becoming fearless, mature, and disciplined as we embrace the Way to our higher destiny.

That's why Saturn's duality is **Dominion/Slavery.** *This is the aspect of consciousness demonstrating whether we are limited or limiting others in helpful or hurtful ways.** By our Saturnian function we are slavers or enslaved, controllers or oppressed, and through these experiences come to a patient and mature conscious participation in the Great Work, rejecting lesser things and actively accepting higher responsibilities and higher work to help the world.

While Jupiter's quality of radical expansion always envisions limitless larger vistas of possibility, an unbounded Jupiter continually moves us in too many directions to be effective in any of them. While Saturn binds us under pressure, it also demonstrates our power to shape forms over time using skill, patience, and organization.

♄ Saturn: Spiritual Master, Spiritual Friend

The Planetary Dualities		
Sun	Fruitfulness	Sterility
Moon	Peace	Strife
Mercury	Life	Death
Venus	Wisdom	Folly
Mars	Grace	Sin
Jupiter	Wealth	Poverty
Saturn	Dominion	Slavery

---

*Paul Foster Case, *The Tarot: A Key to the Wisdom of the Ages,* (Macoy Publishing Co. 1947) 40, 50, 58,119, 161. 181, 196

♄ Saturn: Spiritual Master, Spiritual Friend

TRANSMUTING NEGATIVE PLANETARY EXPRESSIONS

We can only come to a solid individuality by using all the tools at our disposal. These are indicated by all the astrological factors in our charts. While we are somewhat bound by the limits of how our planets function, we simultaneously have the Divine power to transcend the limitations of all our planets and signs and use each of them in the right way and time to reveal who we really are and why we're here on Earth.

In the cosmic scheme of things, Saturn is the outermost of the "Sacred Seven" visible planets. This symbolizes its function of setting boundaries, as well as the limits we must work within if we are ever to transcend those limitations. Saturn teaches us what we are forced to confront before we break past our inner and outer limits into the spiritual realms of Uranus, Neptune, Pluto, and TransPluto. The outer quartet of invisible planets, Uranus, Neptune, Pluto, and TransPluto do not have a dual quality, since they symbolize transpersonal energies working together and synergistically, with each an aspect of the four-fold Divine Energy Force beyond the boundaries of the known.

To recap, each of the seven visible planets represents factors in the personality, and each of them has healthy and unhealthy ways of manifesting. By understanding the dual functions of the seven visible "sacred" planets, we can more easily assess the energies in play in our lives and the lives of others in any experience. Any time a trait associated with one of these dual functions presents itself as a problem, we can antidote and transmute the situation through applying the appropriate planetary solution to the dysfunctional behavior. For example, if we are with someone trapped in a state of fear or victimization, then we antidote the situation by understanding and/or demonstrating maturity and the correct "command and control" expression to

39

♄ Saturn: Spiritual Master, Spiritual Friend

transmute the negativity.

In another example, if we find ourselves impoverished, it is a Jupiter issue, since the problem is wealth not coming forth. The antidote involves releasing any sense of neediness, and finding a more abundant view of the possibilities. If it seems our best efforts are bringing decay and not life-affirming results, it's a Mercury issue. By changing our mental state, or Mercury function, we come out of perceptions and opinions creating patterns of activity leading to decay or death, and come into recognizing how to see life-affirming approaches which open possibilities rather than deny or frustrate the potential.

You can see how you can apply these solutions to problems of interpersonal living and communication. If you're trying to have a discussion with someone and what they're saying is undermining your confidence in your hopes, dreams, truth or experience, then affirm the life, light, and understanding you've found in your experience, truth, hopes and dreams. By staying focused on your strengths, clarity, and ability to give life to your ideas, you don't allow any decaying toxic Mercury expression by others to influence you in negative ways.

This is why it is very important NOT to agree with another's toxic point of view simply to be polite. To agree with a toxic view affirms what we really don't want to affirm. In responding to toxic views and attitudes, we usually don't want to attack them, since using Mars interpersonally often creates antagonism and can result in as much error and missing the mark as it does truth. While we all need to sharpen our wits from time to time in vigorous discussions about life and its lessons, an excess of Mars often creates contention.

However, if we find an appropriate higher way of expressing Venus, it usually will lead us to wisdom rather than folly. This way we find desired beneficial outcomes helping us overcome many difficulties in human relations, both by avoiding certain traps and securing forms of beauty. Knowing which planetary energies are in play, and which are needed to facilitate favorable results, is how we

40

♄ Saturn: Spiritual Master, Spiritual Friend

learn and teach the wisdom we know.

On a related note, in Medical Astrology there are two ways posited to deal with planetary dysfunction. One applies opposite planet or sign antidotes to counter the problem. The other applies more of the same planetary energy, substituting the higher positive function for the lower. "Fighting fire with fire" is only one way of describing the second approach. Specific antidotes are usually determined by whether something is in excess or deficiency, and whether diminishment or "jumpstarting" is appropriate. As we learn the value of applying different energies in different situations, we learn there are many possible ways to solve problems.

The Spiritual Quartet ♅ ♆ ♇ ♇ or ⯝

Uranus, Neptune, Pluto, and TransPluto symbolize the transpersonal elements in existence, and represent spiritual energies challenging us to bring forth our highest Self via large scale collective forces affecting all individuals within their respective transcendent realms. The outermost spiritual planets symbolize forces "beyond individual control," and affect all of us simultaneously.

Since most of us have relatively little ability to shape how widespread Divine energies will manifest in collective consciousness, we have to learn how to respond to these transpersonal forces the best we are able. We do this through mastering the functions of the "Seven Sacred Planets" comprising the components of our personality, since then we can express the best qualities of the spiritual quartet.

After we break through to the other side of the limitations symbolized by Saturn, we are free to

♄ Saturn: Spiritual Master, Spiritual Friend

individualize, experience a transcendent connectedness with all other Life, get to the essence of our spiritual core, and find infinite Grace in redeeming the promise of making our spiritual nature real in the world, consciously living our higher purpose. As we find ways to express the spiritual energies of the transpersonal quartet through the various parts of personality symbolized by the seven visible planets, the outer quartet opens up a much vaster field of spiritual activity, and shows us conditions where we must adapt within the larger field.

Uranus symbolizes our path of Transpersonal Individualization. Through Uranus we find Divine individuality and true autonomy. Uranus represents our originality and genius as a function of our eternal quest, and beckons us to a forever-renewing progressive, independent uniqueness of existence.

Neptune symbolizes our path to Transpersonal Collectivization. Neptune allows us to know through direct experience that we are the merest speck of individualized Light/Life in an infinite field of sentient Light/Life. It is the vehicle by which we experience Oneness of Life, and the perpetuity of eternal connectedness within the One Life.

Pluto symbolizes our path to Transpersonal Transfiguration. Through Pluto we know the purified essence of our spiritual core, and stand fearless as we eliminate all that prevents us from being Divinely transfigured. When we become friends with Pluto, "Lord of the Underworld," we learn how to be forever renewed, stripped of the dross of useless things. Pluto is the Phoenix Firebird, the Pillar of Fire destroying all forms so the essence may be reborn.

TransPluto symbolizes manifestations of "Divine Mother" energy. Through TransPluto we experience the vastness of the Divine Feminine, and through accepting Divine Grace we enter into a vast field of compassionate redemption which brings a new Spring after every symbolic Winter in our lives.

Before we enter the next section, there is one more player in the Cosmic choir involved in how we break free of

℞ Saturn: Spiritual Master, Spiritual Friend

certain ego limitations so we can live "the symbolic life" of transpersonal significance. Chiron symbolizes our Divine mentor who helps us heal our woundedness and become our Higher Self. In mythology, Chiron was said to be the first and best centaur with similar virtues as Thoth-Hermes. As Chiron is beyond Saturn, that part of our Divine Life serves to bridge the boundaries symbolized by Saturn and guides us into the Transpersonal realms.

Chiron mentors us so we may heal and venture beyond the boundaries of Saturn, and serves to bridge the edge of our limitations and the eternal need for individualization associated with Uranus. As we embrace the quest of this eternally wandering mentor and healer, we are no longer bound by local conditions, ignorance, taboos, assumptions, and superstitions, and heal various wounds along the road of Life to become the living manifestation of our Higher Self. Our healed Higher Self then becomes the vehicle to express our true nature as eternal Soul/Spirits living in the world of the five senses and the mind.

THE PLANETARY OCTAVES

There is said to be a specific relationship between several of the inner planets and the Transpersonal planets. These relationships are important in understanding how the worldly and spiritual functions are bridged in our charts, and offers another perspective on the dictum "As Above So Below." As we refine and master the expression of the inner planets, we make them suitable vehicles for the expression of the Outer Quartet of spiritual energies we have at our disposal.

Welcome to the world of planetary octaves! Though there are some variances in what I'm about to offer you, this is the generally accepted theory of octave relationships between the visible and invisible planets. Traditionally, we are told Mercury is the "lower octave" of Uranus, and

℞ Saturn: Spiritual Master, Spiritual Friend

Uranus is the "higher octave" of Mercury. We are told Venus is the "lower octave" of Neptune, and Neptune is the "higher octave" of Venus. And we are told Mars is the "lower octave" of Pluto, and Pluto is the "higher octave" of Mars.

It is easy to see the correlations here, since Mercury is the coordinating mental function through which we explore and learn all the knowledge there is to learn, while Uranus is the synthesizing, creative, individualizing part of our spiritual nature. Mercury explores, evaluates, categorizes, and assimilates knowledge, while Uranus allows us to weave all we discover into a truly individual form of expressing our unique way of realizing and applying the knowledge we've found.

Venus is the aesthetic principle, the part of us which attunes to people, art, beauty, and all the things we like in any given period of life. Neptune represents broad, amorphous concepts that are "in fashion," those things, behaviors, and ideas that appeal to a larger collectivity and take ten thousand shapes. As we learn to express our Venus function ever more perfectly, we can bring into manifestation what is appealing or pleasing to many.

Mars is how we use highly energetic force in focused, pointed ways, cutting through binding things, conditions, and circumstances. Through its assertiveness and skills in "attack and defense," Mars leads us to become good spiritual warriors in any field of activity. Pluto represents the force of absolute transformation, and those events by which we die to an old life and are reborn to a new one. As we refine our Mars expression, we become agents through whom the transformational process may move its magic and cut through obstacles and obstructions in the process.

From one point of view, these are not separate energies, since they all reside within all of us, each to be realized and practiced in the right place and time. As we develop, expand, and refine how we express Mercury, Venus, and Mars energies, we naturally build the bridge to mastering our expression of how Uranus, Neptune, and

♄ Saturn: Spiritual Master, Spiritual Friend

Pluto operate in and through us. This is where Saturn, the gatekeeper and spiritual Friend who offers us different disciplines to develop different skills, is all important in the process of evolving from limited abilities to mastering all our inner functions.

Over time and experience, Saturn helps us train Mercury not to be scattered and unfocused, allowing our mental function to move beyond old limitations of mind so we can express our uniqueness. Saturn helps us train Venus not to be superficial, vain, and self-preoccupied, allowing our expression of what's beautiful or valuable to move beyond old limitations to express the beauty of a larger ideal. Saturn helps us train Mars not to be impulsive, abrasive, or needlessly destructive, allowing our ability to act to be in perfect alignment with the transformational need of the moment.

Our Mercury, Venus, and Mars, when trained by Saturn, allow us to express higher transpersonal principles as an ongoing process of perfection in ever changing circumstances. With each turn of life's wheel, we are offered opportunities to come to even greater realizations of how to apply our personal energies to express transpersonal spiritual intention, or be the spiritual antidote to the worldly problems presenting themselves in a given place or time. However, there is another octave relationship never explored before now that offers major implications for those of us who live in the 21st century.

Because we have a Spiritual Quartet, and not simply a Spiritual Triad, we have a fourth octave relationship involving Jupiter and TransPluto, with the former the lower octave, and the latter the higher octave. As we briefly discussed, TransPluto is the ultimate spiritual redemptive force, the protective Divine Grace blessing all that is good, true, and beautiful. TransPluto nurtures these qualities across vast sweeps of time in all sentient Beings. They find expression through the planet Jupiter, the worldly representative of good, true, merciful, and protective energies blessing us to go forth in the world to ever greater "experiments in truth."

℞ Saturn: Spiritual Master, Spiritual Friend

So each time we realize a greater way to express our Jupiter, those energies become the vehicle through which we may become the embodiment of Divine Mother energy in the world. As our Jupiter function evolves to its highest, best manifestation, we can become the living expression of redemption, blessing, protection, or grace in those worldly affairs where our karma allows us the opportunity. Once we have refined our Mercury, Venus, Mars, and Jupiter into adequate living vehicles to express spiritual energy, we can demonstrate the power of Uranus, Neptune, Pluto or TransPluto as we are called to do so.

THE TWELVE SIGNS

In astrology, there are twelve signs representing the "whole cycle" of experience. The sequence is Aries, Taurus, Gemini, Cancer, Leo, Virgo, Libra, Scorpio, Sagittarius, Capricorn, Aquarius, and Pisces.

These twelve signs each have special qualities and a mode of expression. The quality of the signs is indicated by the four elements, those being Fire, Earth, Air, and Water. The Fire signs are said to be aspirational, inspired, brightening, idealistic, freeing, courageous, and assertive. The Earth signs are said to be practical, grounded, utilitarian, industrious, possessive, dependable, and security-minded. The Air signs are said to be associative, relational, mentally active, versatile, detached, expressive, and imaginative. The Water signs are said to be emotional, romantic, devoted, restless, impressionable, and sensitive.

Each sign is identified with one of the elements. Aries, Leo, and Sagittarius are the Fire signs. Taurus, Virgo, and Capricorn are the Earth signs. Gemini, Libra, and Aquarius are the Air signs. Cancer, Scorpio, and Pisces are the Water signs.

Each sign also has its mode of expression. There are three modes of expression: Cardinal (activating), Fixed (stabilizing), and Mutable (distributive). The Cardinal signs

♄ Saturn: Spiritual Master, Spiritual Friend

initiate activity. The Fixed signs stabilize action in consistent forms which resist change. The Mutable signs adapt, break up, and distribute energy.

Cardinal signs are independent, pioneering, active-expressive, forceful, original, and very much in the present. Fixed signs are stable, conserving, persistent, reliable, dependable, firm, passive, and very much into perpetuating what has been. Mutable signs are adaptable, flexible, versatile, imitative, dualistic, restless, and very future oriented.

As you can see, this combination of four elements spread across three modes of operation creates twelve possible forms of sign expression. The Fire signs are followed by Earth signs. Earth signs are followed by Air signs, Air signs are followed by Water signs. Water signs are followed by Fire signs. This sequence is consistent throughout the Zodiac.

The other consistent sequence is the Cardinal signs are followed by Fixed signs. Fixed signs are followed by Mutable signs. Mutable signs are followed by Cardinal signs, with this pattern repeating as we proceed around the Zodiac. This gives us three signs of each element and four signs sharing similar modes of action.

That yields the "firing sequence" of the signs: Aries (Cardinal Fire) is followed by Taurus (Fixed Earth), followed by Gemini (Mutable Air). Cancer (Cardinal Water) is followed by Leo (Fixed Fire), followed by Virgo (Mutable Earth). Libra (Cardinal Air) is followed by Scorpio (Fixed Water), followed by Sagittarius (Mutable Fire). Capricorn (Cardinal Earth) is followed by Aquarius (Fixed Air), followed by Pisces (Mutable Water). Each of these phases of reality is important in itself and all of them together show us how the twelve stages of our never ending journey through the various sign experiences unfold in an orderly sequence.

♄ Saturn: Spiritual Master, Spiritual Friend

The Four Elements			
Fire Signs	Aries	Leo	Sagittarius
Earth Signs	Taurus	Virgo	Capricorn
Air Signs	Gemini	Libra	Aquarius
Water Signs	Cancer	Scorpio	Pisces

The Three Modes of Expression				
Cardinal	Aries	Cancer	Libra	Capricorn
Fixed	Taurus	Leo	Scorpio	Aquarius
Mutable	Gemini	Virgo	Sagittarius	Pisces

PLANETARY SIGN RULERSHIPS

The seven visible planets all have two signs they are said to "rule." This means they are "at home" in those signs, and have their natural expression in those signs. The Sun and Moon work together and rule Cancer and Leo. Mercury rules Gemini and Virgo, Venus rules Taurus and Libra, and Mars rules Aries and Scorpio. Jupiter rules Sagittarius and Pisces, and Saturn rules Capricorn and Aquarius. The planets of the Spiritual Quartet also have signs they rule (Libra through Taurus), but I regard them more as the spiritual rulers of those signs, while the Sacred Seven are the worldly rulers of those signs.

ƕ Saturn: Spiritual Master, Spiritual Friend

WORLDLY AND SPIRITUAL RULERSHIPS

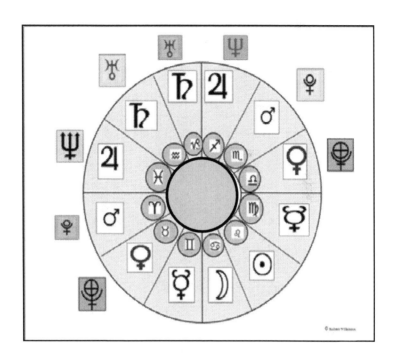

♄ Saturn: Spiritual Master, Spiritual Friend

When any planet is in the sign opposite the one they rule, they are said to be in "exile," considered to be a detriment or debility in traditional astrology. I have found no planet in any sign is inherently "bad" since all the planets have both a healthy as well as unhealthy expression, regardless of their sign position. A planet in exile may operate expertly outside its natural comfort zone, even in "unnatural" circumstances, where that planetary function is perfect for the situation.

Besides the signs of their "home" and "exile," all the planets have a sign said to be their "exaltation," with the opposite sign called their "fall." Here again we must get beyond judging a planetary position as "good" or "bad." A planet in a sign of exaltation merely means it's in its "sign of greatest growth," whereas a planet's "fall" merely means it's in a "sign where growth is not optimal." Does it mean something "bad?" Not necessarily, because it's ultimately about the healthy or unhealthy function of the planet and how we express those energies.

HOW THE PLANETS EXPRESS THROUGH THE SIGNS

♈ ♉ ♊ ♋ ♌ ♍ ♎ ♏ ♐ ♑ ♒ ♓

Our planetary lights shine through the filters represented by the twelve signs. The Sun in Aries is illuminated by Aries people, events, and ways of being. Sun in Taurus is illuminated by Taurus people, events, and ways of being. Sun in Cancer is illuminated by Cancer people, events, and ways of being. Sun in Libra is illuminated by Libra people, events, and ways of being.

The light of the Sun finds form through the Moon. The Moon reflects the Light/Life of our "solar system of

ℏ Saturn: Spiritual Master, Spiritual Friend

personality traits." Moon in Leo reflects and feels in Leo ways. Moon in Sagittarius reflects and feels in Sagittarius ways. Moon in Pisces reflects and feels in Pisces ways.

Taking a brief look at the other components of personality, as we discussed earlier, Mercury shows how we coordinate various life affairs and the different areas of our personality. Mercury in Gemini coordinates in Gemini ways. Mercury in Leo coordinates in Leo ways. Mercury in Scorpio coordinates in Scorpio ways.

Venus is what we like, appreciate, and value. Venus in Taurus likes and values Taurus people, music, art, and experiences; Venus in Aquarius likes and values Aquarius people, music, activities, and experiences. Venus in Pisces likes and values Pisces people, music, art, and experiences.

As noted earlier, Mars is how we "attack the problems of life," how we mobilize, and what aggravates us. Mars in Gemini is moved to act along multiple lines at once, and often engages a battle of ideas. Mars in Cancer is moved to act cautiously with an eye to not taking chances as they secure and feel their way through each step of their plan. Mars in Libra acts in a balanced moderate way, and always takes multiple considerations into account before they act.

Jupiter in Aries finds opportunities in Aries ways and places, such as pioneering endeavors, or where we must act on our own impulses without others interfering with our initiatives. Jupiter in Libra finds opportunities in Libra ways and places, such as cooperative endeavors and adventures, or those opportunities requiring nuance or diplomacy. Jupiter in Aquarius finds opportunities in Aquarius ways and places, such as large scale projects requiring team work, or those involving forms of "world service."

Our Saturn sign shows us the experiences leading us through and beyond limitations so we learn to respond maturely and effectively. Saturn is also our "bottom line," what we can and cannot live with. I'll explain more in the next chapter. In any case, regardless of the sign a planet is

♄ Saturn: Spiritual Master, Spiritual Friend

in, there are strengths and skills to be cultivated, and hindrances and malfunctions to overcome.

Each chart is unique, since each planetary position has its unique relationship to all the other planets in a chart. A Sun sign late in a month operates differently than a Sun sign from early in a month or the middle of the month. Just like cars and wine, each year is a unique "vintage," and each part of the year has its special qualities.

For example, a Virgo Sun in one year may have its ruler Mercury in Leo, while another year it might be in Virgo or Libra, or any two of the above, since Mercury often moves fast and changes signs very quickly. At some point each year, Jupiter advances to the next sign, and Mars could be anywhere. Usually it's only the outer planets (Saturn and the Spiritual Quartet) that show any consistency between successive years and even then, they too move and shift, whether within a sign or between signs.

HOW THE PLANETS EXPRESS THROUGH THE HOUSES

The houses, or the twelve sectors of the chart wheel, are the areas of our life activities: self, both the physical body and the view of reality (1st house, or Ascendant), money and values (2nd house), environment and siblings (3rd house), home and family (4th house, or IC/Nadir), children and creativity (5th house), health, work, and service, (6th house), partnerships and equal relationships (7th house, or Descendant), desires, losses, and magnetism (8th house), philosophy and spiritual views

♄ Saturn: Spiritual Master, Spiritual Friend

(9th house), profession and public standing (10th house, or Midheaven), friends and goals (11th house), and motives, harvests, contemplations, and "self-undoing behaviors" (12th house). There are many more life areas assigned to the houses for those who are interested in exploring further.

The same principle to understanding the planets in the signs applies to the planets in the houses. If the Sun is how we are illuminated and how we illuminate others, the Sun in the 2nd house shows we are illuminated by 2nd house things like money, resources, and values. The Sun in the 7th is illuminated by 7th house things like relationships. Sun in the 11th is illuminated by 11th house things like friendships, goals, and ambitions, as well as group work.

In another example, if Venus is what we like and value, then Venus in the 3rd house finds appreciation and value in their brother-sister relationships and their immediate environment. Venus in the 10th house finds appreciation and value in their profession and public standing, while Venus in the 12th likes and values their solitude and privacy.

If Jupiter is where we find truth and a bigger view, then Jupiter in the 4th house finds these through 4th house associations with home, family, and early life experiences. Jupiter in the 5th house finds these through creativity and children, and Jupiter in the 9th house finds opportunity and truth in higher education, foreign cultures, philosophical-spiritual learning disciplines, and even long distance travel.

A more comprehensive list explaining in greater detail the qualities of the signs, as well as the houses associated with the various parts of life, can be found in numerous astrology books and sites.

♄ Saturn: Spiritual Master, Spiritual Friend

THE ASPECTS

  The aspects (conjunction, sextile, quintile, square, trine, opposition, and many more) are the angular relations between the parts of our personality represented by the planetary positions. In the natal chart, aspects between the planets and angles indicate how the various parts of our nature relate to each other. We can see the harmony between various parts of our nature, or the friction one part of us creates with other parts of us. Most planets make aspects to each other, and these angular relationships between the planets show the phase relationships between all the parts of us, whether natally or via the progressed and transiting aspects.

  For example, the Sun-Saturn aspect in a natal chart (if there is one, since not all planets make aspects to all other planets) indicates how the ability to be illuminated and illuminate others relates to fear and a sense of being bound by circumstances. It shows how those in authority relate to one's Light. A Mercury-Venus aspect reveals how mind relates to likes and dislikes. A Moon-Neptune aspect reveals how the emotions are disposed toward collective consciousness, or timeless, unifying, shared feelings.

  Our Mars-Jupiter aspect is how the natal willingness to act relates to an ability to perceive opportunity or distant possibilities. A Mars-Uranus aspect indicates how our natal genius or individuality can be expressed in direct action. While a planet in a sign and house has distinctive qualities, the aspects it makes and are made to it show the interrelationships between that planetary function and other planetary functions.

  Any aspect is merely one state of relationship between two planets on a continuum of many types of ways they could relate. There are challenging aspects,

♄ Saturn: Spiritual Master, Spiritual Friend

stabilizing aspects, specializing aspects, spiritual aspects, and even aspects indicating various "forks in the road of destiny," where our choices will lead to major life changes. Any aspect can work a number of ways; a frictional aspect can yield beneficial opportunities, or a harmonious aspect can yield a problem.

For example, squares are usually thought to be frictional, but they help us turn corners, as well as put brakes on old ways. Trines can yield understanding and harmony, but also may show an unhealthy internal default position if the two planets are not functioning in a healthy way. A stable harmony between two dysfunctional parts of our personality may not be useful for changing the expression of either. As with the other basic factors in astrology, you can find out more about the aspects and their meaning by consulting any of the vast number of works on the subject.

PROGRESSIONS AND PROGRESSED ASPECTS

When we look at a chart, any thorough analysis involves three factors: the natal (birth) positions, the progressed planetary positions (for those who use progressions), and the transits (where the planets are now) and how they configure with the natal and progressed positions. The natal chart factors are of primary importance since they indicate what was happening when we were born, and represent fundamental patterns we came in with and what we're dealing with our entire life in the way of original equipment.

The natal positions, set at the moment of "first breath," map the innate disposition. Over time these primary predispositions evolve, or "progress." Therefore, they are known as Progressions, a.k.a. "secondary directions." There are also "primary directions," "tertiary directions," and other symbolic ways of calculating how various natal functions evolve over time. They are symbolic

55

♄ Saturn: Spiritual Master, Spiritual Friend

since they are calculated by assuming every day after birth is equivalent to a progressed year. For example, to find progressed positions for when we are 25, in the ephemeris (a book of planetary positions) we count 25 days after our original birthday.

All types of progressions reveal how the natal planets and angles have symbolically moved forward during our lives. Various progressions make angular relationships to the natal positions and each other throughout life, and indicate stages in the process of the evolving inner self, regardless of their relative strength and influence.

Here I'll note many prominent astrologers, including some of the best of the best, never used progressions. I use progressions in my work because I have found them to be valuable in showing our modified inner orientation to the patterns we were born with. They don't override the birth traits, but they reveal different organic tendencies evolving in our inner world. We all have both natal planet and progressed planet tendencies happening at the same time. However, no progression can negate the natal inclinations. To modify is not to nullify. The only way to end a natal tendency is simply to stop doing it.

Progressed aspects to birth planets indicate when those evolved parts of our inner life have hit turning points relative to the natal tendencies, and when our innate and developed ways of expressing ourselves go through a phase shift. Each time a progressed planet moves into another sign, the shift becomes evident, since each sign has its own qualities which are very different than the sign preceding it. By progressions, we see what has fulfilled itself, and can turn to other areas of productive learning and expression.

As you can imagine, our progressed Sun is paramount in clarifying our lives and purpose. As the progressed Sun moves forward through the years, it will make many different aspects to all the planets in our chart. These aspects mark points in our Light/Life where we bring the other planetary functions into "the light of day."

♄ Saturn: Spiritual Master, Spiritual Friend

Our progressed Moon makes all the aspects to all the other planets every 27 years. This shows our evolving feeling experience as it makes every possible phase relationship to every other part of us. Through the progressed Moon we understand how we want to experience life, how we want to live, and what we care about.

Our progressed Mercury, Venus, and Mars also make a variety of aspects with the natal planets, bringing signs, signals, and insights (Mercury), appreciation of the beauty and value of parts of ourselves and our lives (Venus), or the need to mobilize on our own behalf (Mars) as they aspect the other planets. Again, each of these accompany times of inner phase shifts, productive periods, and turning points in how the progressed components of personality relate to the birth self, as well as other evolved parts of personality.

TRANSITING ASPECTS

Transiting aspects are an entirely different matter than progressed aspects. Transiting aspects are dynamic and operate in real time. Transits are where the planets are right now. The transits symbolize the greater "atmosphere" or gestalt within which we live and do our Being, and can be harmonious or frictional with natal traits and how various planetary expressions have evolved.

They affect all parts of the life, from kitty cats to weather patterns to international affairs. That's why the transits are of primary importance. Where the planets were yesterday, are today, and will be tomorrow into eternity symbolize the circumstances happening at those times. Transits indicate what's going on in the moment, from the most personal affairs to the vast field of transpersonal and planetary factors over which we have no control. They operate outside of natal and progressed factors, and generate infinite and complex changing relationships unto

♄ Saturn: Spiritual Master, Spiritual Friend

themselves.

Through transits we can come to understand why events are as they are, whether we helped to create those events or not. There are many situations we encounter throughout life which were created by others and are not under our personal control. Those are the times the only control we have is how we will respond to those factors.

Whether the fusions and beginnings of conjunctions, the polarizations and realizations of oppositions, the gifts and specializations of quintiles, the turning points of squares, or other angles marking phases of our personal evolution as well as larger cycles of change in the world, we can see when it's time to hold or release, as well as initiate, preserve, or transform.

While transiting inner planet aspects are associated with the passing affairs of daily and weekly life, transiting outer planets help us reshape our responses to our "Truth of Being," our Higher Self, and the eternal process of transformation. Outer planet transits take place over a longer time span than inner planet transits, and during those transits we undergo profound personal transformations.

Outer planet aspects to our chart are times when we are taken to the limit of our ability to deal with events beyond individual control. A Pluto transit may accompany a death, but also be a time of radical transformation into our Highest Self. A Neptune transit may accompany a sense of drifting or being lost in life, but it can also be a time of transcendent connectedness with the world and all of life.

A Uranus transit can accompany jarring events and life revolutions, but also awaken us to a path to freedom and liberation from ego-limitations. A Saturn transit may accompany hard realizations, but with the right view we can turn them to good results in reshaping our personality to bring it in line with our highest intentions and purposes. Any aspect can be used wisely or not. It all depends on our point of view and the specific responses we choose.

As the transits make various aspects to our natal and progressed planets, we are either blessed or

58

♄ Saturn: Spiritual Master, Spiritual Friend

challenged by circumstances to respond the best we're able, and bring forth the most positive and effective manifestation of those planetary traits. All transits show us various phases of where we're at with who we are, who we've become, and what we're here to bring forth in our worldly existence. Sometimes an aspect can bring echoes of other times and challenges, which is why each time an aspect occurs it creates the potential of reinforcing a prior response pattern, or the creation of a new response pattern.

This brings up an important point; just because an aspect is over does not mean it's no longer an influence. All we have experienced leaves an impression. Once we go through any aspect and respond to those energies, it establishes a tendency within us. As the tendency is formed and repeated, it becomes a habit. That habit is how we respond to life events.

HOW ASPECTS WORK

Aspects are made by all the progressed and transiting planets to the natal and progressed positions. Some aspects pass quickly, such as those made by faster planets such as Mercury and Venus. Others pass more slowly, such as those made by Mars, Jupiter, and Saturn. Each of these brings their own unique lessons, depending on their specific planetary department of labor.

While all planetary aspects "mean something," as I noted earlier in this chapter, the planets do not "make anything happen." In this sense, we cannot experience a windfall a) if the natal planets do not indicate such a thing, and b) if we are somehow not cooperating with whatever could have brought us the windfall under other circumstances.

Another key principle to keep in mind is when a major life event occurs, you will definitely find a combination of aspects. But a combination of aspects does

♄ Saturn: Spiritual Master, Spiritual Friend

not necessarily indicate something will happen, at least at that time. Some things can be set up by aspects which don't trigger for months or years, or perhaps never if the person decides to scuttle those lines of endeavor.

While the inner planet transits make many aspects over a short time, the aspects of the outermost planets stay active for many months, and sometimes years. They show larger cycles of change and transformation, and as I noted earlier, symbolize conditions over which we have no control except how we will choose to respond to those large scale challenges and opportunities.

For example, one client was very worried when Pluto was approaching the conjunction to her Moon, and wanted to know when the influence would be done. Often the aspects of Pluto (and Saturn!) bring up a sense of dread when they approach a planet in a chart. This is because Saturn is associated with all we fear that limits us, and Pluto is associated with radical transformation, loss of old ways of living, and even annihilation of much of what we believe. It's no wonder people's attention gets very focused during such transits!

During the times Pluto approaches a planet, it's purification time for those parts of our inner nature, where we eliminate what we no longer need symbolized by that planet. Yet, for all Pluto takes away, it also helps us sprout long term seeds of the core of our spiritual essence, which is crucial if we would become our Higher Self.

When transiting Pluto begins to make an aspect to a natal planet, it is as though something of extraordinary importance, even ominous, feels like it's coming. When Pluto makes an exact aspect to a planet, we're in the heart of its influence, for good or ill. When the aspect is separating, its influence is still at work, but with more of a sense something is passing which impacted our life profoundly. However, the influence, even though it's passing, is still with us.

Because life, understanding, and the wisdom we must distill from experience are an unbroken continuum from the angle of higher consciousness, the influences of

♄ Saturn: Spiritual Master, Spiritual Friend

the transiting (and progressed) planets are not separate from those experiences. A Pluto square impacts life in profound ways. Just because it's separating does not mean we are free of its influence, since even a closely separating aspect is still very much a part of our life experience.

A planetary transit indicates something in external reality is getting our attention. Again, the inner planet transits symbolize quickly passing elements of existence, whereas the outer planet transits symbolize slower, more important elements of life. As we respond to the transits, we shape how we deal with those things in the future.

Because the natal planets symbolize the inner "lights," they show the divisions in our life and personality where we "shine out" the inclinations indicated by the sign expression those planets are in. A planetary transit impacts the part of our life represented by the planet it touches, as well as how we demonstrate our innate (natal) planetary energy. And yet, we always have the ability to change our pattern of response, regardless of whether we're dealing with the supposed difficulty of a transiting Saturn square to one of our planets or the supposed benefit of a Jupiter trine to another.

Following up on the previous example of transiting Pluto aspects, as we deal with forming aspects before they become exact, we quicken in anticipation of the challenge, change, understanding, or specializing influence indicated by the aspect being formed. When we are in the heart of an exact aspect, we may or may not find it being dramatically expressed in our outer life, but we are making decisions, whether we know it or not, about how we will respond and express that energy.

By the time an aspect is passing, our lives are moving forward in some way symbolized by that aspect. But it does not mean the aspect is no longer influencing us, since every experience we have impacts our future responses. This is why it's folly to dread approaching hard aspects or rejoice once they are done, since an aspect merely represents the learning path through what we

♄ Saturn: Spiritual Master, Spiritual Friend

confront in the planetary energies being revealed. We will explore these concepts in greater depth later in this book.

RETROGRADE PLANETS ℞

All planets go retrograde as a function of their orbits except the Sun and Moon. What does the term "retrograde" actually mean? All planets speed up and then slow down in their orbital speed relative to the Sun and Earth. This is also true for the Moon, but we don't call it retrogradation.

The Sun seems to speed up or slow down a little based in the sign it's in relative to the Earth. Of course, it's actually the Earth speeding up or slowing down in its orbit, based in whether it's at perihelion (closest to the Sun) or aphelion (farthest away from the Sun) in its orbit.

Due to the way perception works from our angle of vision here on Earth, all the planets from Mercury out to TransPluto go retrograde at regular intervals. Mercury is retrograde three or four times a year, Venus every 18 months, and Mars every 26 months, more or less. The planets from Jupiter out all go retrograde once a year for several months. These are times when the planets seem to be going backward instead of forward in motion.

Planets obviously do not go backwards, but because they slow down and speed up in their orbits relative to the Sun and the Earth, it creates interesting perspectives from our angle of viewing the planets. The best analogy to describe the retrograde motion would be like a slow train appearing to go backward relative to an express train. While both trains are moving forward, looking at a slow train from the window of a fast train makes it seem like the slow train is going backward in motion.

A retrograde re-traces ground already covered once by that planet. First, the planet crosses a sector of the zodiac as it moves forward through the signs. Then

62

♄ Saturn: Spiritual Master, Spiritual Friend

when it retrogrades, it moves back across a part of that same span again, retracing its path across degree points it recently transited before it went retrograde. Then when a retrograde is done and the planet goes direct in motion it again moves across the same span of degrees, which becomes an area of importance in our lives, since we get three experiences of that part of the zodiacal reality. After that, it moves forward until its next retrograde.

All retrogrades help us integrate information as we move forward in our lives and affairs. Some parts of our evolution move forward quickly as the planets move forward in motion through the signs. But then at some point, they slow down and we get a new look at ground already covered. Then when they resume forward motion, it symbolizes a time when we can take what we learned, then re-learned, or viewed and reviewed, and apply those lessons in new ways.

In its orbit, Mercury (mind, the coordinating principle) makes the most number of retrogrades. It speeds up for a while, then slows down for a while, then speeds up again, then slows down again in an eternal dance of racing forward to get new information, then slowing to reconsider the information it just received. We can apply this speeding up and slowing down to other planets as well. The type of information depends on which planet is involved.

For example, when Venus is direct in motion we get Venusian "information." Then when it slows down and goes retrograde we get a different view of what we just learned about those energies. When Mars goes retrograde, it slows the forward momentum of our direct action. It may be a good time to re-do, re-work, or re-evaluate the plan or method of doing something. These are good times to slow one set of activities down and accomplish other things until it's time to pick up the pace on the original actions.

Transiting planets going retrograde and making repeated aspects to another planet are a common occurrence. When Mercury, Venus, and Mars go retrograde, they all make aspects when direct in motion

63

℞ Saturn: Spiritual Master, Spiritual Friend

and approaching the retrograde point. Then when retrograde they make many of the same aspects, especially to the outer planets. When they go direct, they make those aspects a third time. What does this mean?

When a planet makes an aspect and then moves forward, it symbolizes something about our experience of that phase relationship. Then if it slows down and goes retrograde and makes the same aspect again, we are shown something concerning this phase relationship, but from a different angle of view. When it speeds up and goes direct in motion and again makes an aspect for the third time, we have yet another experience of that type of energetic response.

This gives us periodic points where we get three experiences of the same energy, but from different angles. Through our multiple experiences dealing with recurring aspects, we can synthesize the various ways we've experienced those energies and can bring forth the highest and best response possible.

CHAPTER 3

WHO AND WHAT IS SATURN?

Before we begin our exploration about Saturn's deeper spiritual qualities, we'll take a short look at some of its astronomical and mythological qualities.

SATURN IN ASTRONOMY

Saturn, as we all know, is the outermost of the seven traditional planets of antiquity. Saturn is outside of Jupiter's orbit, and is known for its many rings surrounding the body of the planet. It is the sixth planet from the Sun and is the second largest behind Jupiter. It has a very strong magnetic field, is less dense than water, and generates more power than it receives.

Galileo was the first to observe it by telescope in 1610. Its rings were thought to be unique until 1977, when rings were observed around Uranus, and after that, also around both Jupiter and Neptune. So it seems all the planets from Jupiter out to Neptune have rings, which places these planets in a class unto themselves!

Three of Saturn's rings can be seen from Earth and are composed of ice and other substances. They are brighter than the rings of the other planets, even though they are very thin. Several moons of Saturn act as "shepherd moons" to keep the rings from spreading out.

ℏ Saturn: Spiritual Master, Spiritual Friend

SATURN IN MYTHOLOGY

Saturn was a key player in Babylonian, Etruscan, and Vedic Astrology. In Vedic Astrology, Saturn supposedly judges us on the good and bad we do in life. This makes it clear why it would be associated with the concept of karma, and the consequences of our good or bad behaviors.

Its name comes from the Romans, who believed it to be the god of agriculture. Saturn was considered to be the same as the Greek god Kronos, meaning "time." To the Romans Saturn was also associated with generation, dissolution, wealth, renewal, and liberation. Saturnalia was the festival dedicated to Saturn, which we are told involved feasts, free speech, and gift giving. Because I don't want to reiterate the vast amount of information related to Saturn's role in various mythologies, please reference any number of excellent texts that elaborate on this subject.

SATURN'S QUALITIES

As Saturn moves through all the signs, it reveals various facets of our karmas, as well as the mysterious thing unique to each of us, Dharma, which we'll explore in greater depth in the next chapter. The more we learn about the dance between our inner Saturn and transiting Saturn as the timekeeper in the world of affairs, the clearer will be the path to mastery over our lives as we understand what we came to Earth to learn.

Obviously, in learning how to make Saturn our friend, we learn about Saturn's virtues. We also learn about Saturn's negative qualities, enabling us to use positive Saturn virtues to transmute its difficult side and prevent negativity, pessimism, or rigidity from taking our minds, feelings, and lives where we don't want to go.

As we can infer from Saturn's mythological correspondences, Saturn teaches us the "agricultural"

♄ Saturn: Spiritual Master, Spiritual Friend

principles we are learning in the "Garden of Life." Saturn teaches us perfect timing on when to till the soil of our personalities, when to fertilize, when to plant, when to weed, and when to do "pest control."

Saturn teaches us when to live by the rules and when to suspend them. It teaches when and how to renew our lives, when to give gifts, when to exercise free speech, and when the gates will swing open and we are freed to live a better life. Saturn shows us the path to liberation.

As I mentioned previously, Saturn has the quality of knowing the value of perseverance, reasonable and appropriate limits, adherence to duty, and the ability to respond productively and effectively in the moment. As we cultivate a healthy relationship with those parts of our personality, we learn to demonstrate other positive Saturn qualities such as patience, discipline, organization, patience, structure, maturity, patience, understanding, wisdom, patience, authority, responsibility, and of course, patience.

These are expressions of Saturn's power allowing us to take command of our personalities and lives, and become wise in understanding we are able to do and when. Each of the planets has its lessons and strengths for us to learn and apply, and all those inside the orbit of Saturn are subject to Saturn's binding force and structuring power. Saturn is how we define the limits of our various planetary expressions, as well as how they mature as a function of time.

SATURN – RULER OF CAPRICORN AND AQUARIUS EXALTED IN LIBRA

Saturn is said to "rule" the signs of Capricorn and Aquarius, and is said to be "exalted" in Libra. What does this mean?

The two signs a planet rules show us the dual nature of the planet's qualities. Capricorn is a Cardinal

℞ Saturn: Spiritual Master, Spiritual Friend

Earth (initiating/practical) sign, while Aquarius is a Fixed Air (stable/interactive) sign. So Saturn's nature is to be initiating in its practicality and self-organization, and stable in its associations, aspirations, and ideals. This part of us is able to take the initiative in organizing practical methods in ways we choose, and stabilize ideas and relationships within an idealistic frame of reference.

Because Saturn's nature includes both Capricorn and Aquarius, it also includes all the other types of the Earth and Air elements. That means that Saturn also has the Earth qualities of Taurus and Virgo, the other Earth signs, as well as the Air elements of Gemini and Libra, the other Air signs.

Earth has the quality of determination, never yielding an inch if it doesn't need to. It has the quality of knowing how to adjust to circumstances on its own terms to achieve maximum effectiveness or leverage. It has the quality of seeing many ways to understand and communicate other possibilities within the larger time-picture, and it really does well when communicating reasonable and balanced views of all side of any issue. While it may take time, a healthy Saturn always finds a fair and just assessment of a situation.

The more you can learn about Capricorn and Aquarius, the better you will understand the nature of Saturn's strengths and weaknesses. These signs are said to govern social order, and how an individual may find personal effectiveness within the larger order. They are aspirational and ambitious in a public rather than private sense, reference their own authority rather than look to others, and always have a sense of high visibility.

Both Capricorn and Aquarius are motivated by protocol and "good policy." We all have all the signs in our astrological charts, and the sectors where we have these energies active show us where we are deliberate in our public expression, especially in situations where we are in the public eye. Both signs have their own sense of protocol, and their expression is governed by the protocols of the situations in which they find themselves.

♄ Saturn: Spiritual Master, Spiritual Friend

Protocols can serve to keep our expression proper and within appropriate boundaries, but they can also stifle spontaneity and individuality. Protocols are essentially the customs and regulations of formal, worldly interactions, and place great value on diplomacy, formality, precedents, rules of behaviors, and social-cultural mores. These are all facets of Saturn's nature. The trick to mastering the Saturn part of our personality is knowing when protocols serve a higher purpose, and knowing when they must be stretched, bent, or discarded altogether as inadequate for achieving our higher purpose in the moment. By accepting our power of practical initiative as well as the power to structure or restructure a synthesized overview of things, we come to understand what worked yesterday may not work today, and what works today may not tomorrow. Saturn allows us to shape methods as we need to while keeping our long term self-interest in view.

Saturn is said to be "exalted" in the Cardinal Air sign of Libra. A planet's sign of exaltation indicates that sign energy is the arena of greatest growth for that planetary function. This implies Saturn finds its best expression as it embodies and expresses the qualities of Libra, an energy that takes the initiative in trying to relate to others in ideal ways..

Libra exemplifies the qualities of justice, fairness, balance, and equipoise. Libra is about finding the many nuanced ways of approaching the various shadings of any given thing. It is not that Libra is necessarily perfectly balanced or centered in some internal equilibrium, but it searches for the perfect equilibrium and perfectly balanced perspective in every situation.

Libra is the part of us able to act of its own initiative to find an appropriate self-direction. It is the sign of idealistic spiritual virtues representing those actions bringing us harmony or disharmony through which we come to a perfect balance in view and action through a multitude of minor adjustments.

Its symbol is the scales, representing its "weighing and judging" quality. Through Libra we measure action to

♄ Saturn: Spiritual Master, Spiritual Friend

determine if the perfect proportion has been achieved. When we achieve an ideal expression of this energy, we eliminate hesitancy and indecision, and direct our actions with discernment and elegance. It is the means by which we translate knowledge into action as we direct the course of our relationships and choose our opportunities with deliberation and calculated foresight.

Saturn leads us to master our spiritual equilibrium through various life experiences. Spiritual equilibrium, a.k.a. equipoise, is something we all have, but only after we learn to reference the "higher inner" and not the "dense outer." As we master an inner sense of equipoise, we find we are expressing ourselves in many different and balanced ways.

In my own journey to find spiritual equilibrium, I have found not all things can be expressed in perfectly balanced ways, since not all concepts are or need to be "perfectly balanced." It's better to find a mature understanding of why things are structured the way they are (Saturn) than seek an imposed artificial "balance" which may prevent a needed correction. As we examine many different perspectives, we are able to eliminate useless and wasteful considerations. Even though finding the appropriate practicality as well as a balanced sense of proportion involve walking "the razor's edge," I've found these are both conditioned by the eye of the beholder, as well as the level of comprehension.

Libra weighs and judges by looking at everything in terms of opposing perspectives, but can fall prey to considering polarities which may not be equivalent. For example, many people think the antipode, or oppositional energy, to love is hate, when in fact hate masks fear, and as we learn loving responses to these, we find they no longer have any power to affect us. And truly, as we become the greater Love we ARE, we let go of fear and have the power to dispel it. This profound realization taught me a lot about the uselessness of hate and fear, and encouraged me to seek understanding through examining issues from many sides without avoiding what I needed to face.

SATURN AND TIME

As I offered you in Chapter One, Saturn rules time. Time can be understood from many angles of approach, and over time we are afforded opportunities to come to a balanced view of things past and present. Time is also relative, as is exemplified in Einstein's famous statement that "When a man sits with a pretty girl for an hour, it seems like a minute. But let him sit on a hot stove for a minute and it's longer than any hour. That's relativity."

Since time itself is relative, then perhaps Saturn is not the stationary, sclerotic thing we have been led to believe it is, but rather when at its best, a constantly self-adjusting perspective about time and movement through experience. We have an ability to master our responses across time, which means we have dominion over time and ways of experiencing inner and outer reality. Therefore, we can conclude time and experience are pure mental constructs, and not fixed conditions trapping us in 3D reality.

In the present world, time does seem to have sped up from even a few decades ago. I believe since time is inextricably bound to perception, then perhaps as our global perspective has shifted, so has our perception of time. Some of this may be a result of a quickened means of interacting, but perhaps there is also a factor of time speeding up due to the quickening which occurs at the end of an Age, because of the collective expectancy around unknown things yet to come and already in motion.

Certainly our perception of quickened communications has led many in the world to see time differently. We are experiencing a quickening of time because the time gaps in our interactions have shortened thanks to progressive revolutionary developments like the internet, where information can be exchanged globally in just seconds.

Everything is much faster today than even one or two decades ago, and this is influencing our perception of

♄ Saturn: Spiritual Master, Spiritual Friend

time. We're all learning to manage the process of modern existence while living at a much faster pace than previous generations. Saturn can help us find the perfectly balanced sense of perspective and proportion as we use the fourth dimension of time to measure our three dimensional evolutionary experience.

WHAT SATURN TEACHES US

In astrology, we learn each sign is actually one pole in an axis of opposing signs. We also learn that each sign manifests through its own qualities, as well as the qualities of its opposite sign. By knowing the health or dysfunction of a sign expression, we can find antidotes to problems associated with those signs.

Because Saturn and the Sun/Moon rule opposing signs, it implies the antidotes to a problematic Saturn are positive Solar and Lunar qualities, regardless of which signs these occupy in a chart. If we feel fear (Saturn), we learn to generate courage (Sun) or find a self-nurturing security (Moon). If we feel dull or uninspired (Saturn) we are challenged to find a creative outlet we can pour our hearts into (Sun), or something we can help to grow (Moon). If we feel trapped (Saturn), we learn to see the whole picture of our "personal solar system" and ways to "rule our realm" (Sun) and find significant personal forms we care about (Moon) to see what can be done and when.

Saturn's discipline becomes a great comfort when we finally accept both our limits in the moment, as well as the flexibility of those limits when approached from different angles of understanding. It seems the security of knowing how much power we have to shape our responses to various challenges is the comfort we find while navigating life's changes.

I found it useful to see Saturn as "the reason things are the way they are," which gave me the benefit of not being so surprised by life's unanticipated challenges. It

♄ Saturn: Spiritual Master, Spiritual Friend

allowed me to suspend judgment as I sought understanding without falling into a rut of victim consciousness or other unhelpful states of mind. Even when unexpected or sudden events occurred, as I embraced Saturn's virtues of patience, maturity, and self-discipline, I found it resulted in a sense of power to steer the process, even while navigating difficult waters.

Saturn keeps us on track when all else seems to fail. Saturn keeps us persevering when all hope is lost and all options are exhausted. Saturn is our determination to keep going until we get to the other side of any ordeal. Saturn is persistence. Saturn hangs in there. Saturn is not dissuaded by any external thing. Saturn is the power that persists in and through time.

As a function of bringing forth wisdom through direct experience, Saturn teaches us to search for the pearl of understanding in the midst of challenging circumstances. Saturn may be associated with harsh conditions and limitations, but over time it teaches us to change our view of what is possible when we are in circumstances bringing us pain or creating a state of suffering.

Saturn is associated with any sense of loneliness we may experience as we live life. When we feel lonely, we are given a perfect opportunity to transmute that unhelpful emotion into an understanding of the blessings of solitude and the reality we are always totally and completely connected to "All-That-Is."

Saturn experiences bring the opportunities allowing us to demonstrate mature self-love, self-discipline, and a healthy sense that some limits are good and necessary if we are to be led to beneficial harvests. It shows us how to use free will to shape our future.

♄ Saturn: Spiritual Master, Spiritual Friend

SATURN IS OUR BOTTOM LINE

While we can shrug off many things, there are other challenges showing us our "bottom line." Some events push us to the sticking point, where we will go so far and no farther. These show us we've hit a limit, and must choose how to respond productively, regardless of what others think or feel.

Saturn represents the "bottom line" when it comes to what we can and cannot live with, and what we believe is in our self-interest. Saturn is what delineates the boundaries of our responsibilities as we know them to be, apart from what others assume or insist they are. Once we're at peace with our inner Saturn function, we know a balanced and wise approach to life, have no problem expressing our sense of how much we want to be involved in a given situation, and are secure as we set our own course.

The sign our natal Saturn occupies symbolizes the qualities of our bottom line and how we're learning to live our higher destiny in a conscious way. For example, Saturn in Virgo finds its bottom line through Virgo experiences, while Saturn in Aquarius finds its bottom line through Aquarian experiences. Saturn in Taurus finds its limits and the power of its self-determined authority in Taurus things, experiences, and lessons, whereas Saturn in Pisces finds its bottom line in the realm of Pisces experiences, people, and activities.

Regardless of the sign position of Saturn in our charts, it shows where we dig in and take a hard look at what is absolutely necessary, come to know a sober and pragmatic understanding of what's important, and learn what we need to learn about every lesson that really matters to us. It is the hard edge of what we will and will not tolerate in a situation or with a person, and shows how, when, and where we decide to embrace the self-initiating authorship of our Divine Self.

♄ Saturn: Spiritual Master, Spiritual Friend

This relates back to how we "make Saturn our friend." When we come to peace with what we're here to do, and consciously choose to learn every way we can, then we are comfortable with our process of personal evolution as we shape and reshape our responses over time. Saturn helps us see how to do our Being in ever more effective ways, "taking the high road" (whatever that means to us personally) in a mature and responsible way.

Saturn facilitates our understanding about when we must transcend and let go of certain attitudes while accepting others. Saturn brings us experiences which can lead us to understanding and wisdom, whether we want those experiences or not. Saturn is always present in the lessons we cannot avoid, as well as when we know time's up and we must move forward.

I mentioned earlier that Saturn is usually a factor in those things which frustrate us, because it is associated with the things and events we dread, don't want to deal with, and any sense we have of being trapped within binding circumstances. We can extend this to the binding forces of Nature and Time, since these impose limits on us whether we like it or not, until we choose to take command of the process of Self-realization. Then we're only bound by circumstances until we're not.

We have more power to transmute our deficiencies in the moment than most of us have been led to believe. This power is realized each time we consciously choose a response outside our own and others' presumptions. We are eternally free spirits, and are limited only by the boundaries of our imagination.

THE DANCE OF SATURN AND JUPITER

Saturn dominates any "gathering of planets," since it defines the boundaries of how things function in the world of form. Even when there are transpersonal planets present, Saturn still controls the agenda of all the other

♄ Saturn: Spiritual Master, Spiritual Friend

planets, since it defines the outer limits where the seen meets the unseen, defining what can be done within the larger realm of the visible "solar system" of energies present in a situation.

For example, Jupiter is associated with the lessons we can learn the easy way. Those lessons enable us to imagine greater vistas of development, greater opportunities to extend in time and space, greater life adventures, and greater imagination-driven truths. Saturn, on the other hand, is what slows us down and teaches us structure, discipline, organization, and the most appropriate function in the moment.

Since Jupiter is inside Saturn's orbit, then it is subject to Saturn's binding force and structuring power across time. Saturn gives our Jupiterian imagination the boundaries and structure it needs, and as timekeeper, focuses Jupiter and keeps it from jumping on its horse and riding off in multiple directions simultaneously.

Jupiter and Saturn work together in very important ways showing us the way to take command of the adventure of our lives so it unfolds in a coherent way. As I mentioned earlier, Jupiter is the "cosmic therapist," the part of us that gets a broader view of our psychological issues through the various types of therapists we meet throughout life. This is why Jupiter has an association with shamans, healers, priests, priestesses, and yes, therapists.

Saturn binds and focuses Jupiter's imagination and dreams of endless possibilities. While Jupiter opens the gateways to the promise of a more abundant life adventure, Saturn is what compels us to stick with various types of therapy or healing modalities until we achieve dominion over the fears holding us back from a more perfect self-expression. While Jupiter opens the doors of perception to vaster, freer realities, Saturn keeps us on track until we resolve and release all that hinders us from reclaiming and demonstrating our Divine power.

Jupiter is our imagination of what could be, but through Saturn we find we are still subject to limitations resulting from what we know and what we don't. Through

Saturn we demonstrate our established skills, and find other skills we are still developing. Jupiter leads our imagination into broader vistas that awaken our desire for a larger, more abundant life. However, if a desire is contrary to our higher interests, Saturn is the part of our inner knowing which obstructs us from yielding to those desires which would mess up our lives.

Though Jupiter offers us an abundant life adventure, through Saturn we come to value certain limitations, and the power of persistence and determination in achieving those things which enrich our lives. Even as Jupiter opens the future, Saturn guards the gates to each successive stage of development on our quest to master human existence. We'll discuss the spiritual dimensions of Saturn in the next two chapters.

SATURN DEFINES OUR CREATIVE EXPRESSION

Saturn represents how we choose to define our personal reality. All the inner planets show us parts of that reality, from our innermost experience (the Moon) to the limits of where our fear rubs up against our freedom (Saturn). While we often have little or no ability to create or change the external factors of the reality in which we find ourselves, Saturn allows us to shift focus, method, and how we experience life situations based in a more mature understanding of how we are and are not limited by those external factors.

We can only live the life we are able to create. Saturn is the guardian of binding our creative process in specific forms over specific periods of creative self-expression. We always have the power to transcend the boundaries of our self-expression, since they are not static, but completely defined by personal biases forged within the social and cultural matrix. We always have the ability to choose to step outside our biases and limitations, and embrace the journey of self-reinvention by not assuming

77

that the limits of the past need be the limits of the present or future.

Even though Uranus, Neptune, Pluto, and TransPluto symbolize vast transpersonal spiritual energies affecting everyone through "forces beyond our control," Saturn as the gatekeeper between the visible and the invisible gives us the power to bridge between our worldly existence with our spiritual possibilities. As we explore the boundary where our fear meets our mastery, we move through the grinding zone where ego assumptions and biases collide with our eternal quest for freedom and conscious spiritual individuation. However, once we embrace the lessons of mastering our lower ego, we have the ability to be fully conscious in choosing how we want to respond to larger forces of change in the world.

Through Saturn, we bring all the factors of inner and outer existence under the discipline of our intelligent wisdom. No external thing can prevent us from taking command of how we choose to navigate our life changes, nor strip us of the ability to choose to improve our personality vehicles to manifest the Higher Self and our Soul/Spirit. We are the Way, Truth, and Life/Light we seek. Finding these within, there is no external thing that can prevent us from embodying these eternal verities.

CHARACTER IS DESTINY

Saturn is said to have an association with the number seven, the number of destiny. Thus Saturn is associated with the seven colors of the spectrum, seven tones of the western musical scale, the seven chakras in the human body, the seven planes of existence from the densest to the most spiritual, and seven Rays of Divine energy pervading our planetary system. Each of these manifestations is bound within the secret of the number seven. In number theory seven is the total number of possible expressions of the Divine Triad, and represents

♄ Saturn: Spiritual Master, Spiritual Friend

the perfected work as it has been accomplished in the seven stages of creation.

Creation is a series of stages where each part of the work unfolds organically over time. There are the metaphoric "six days of labor," with the seventh stage the synthesis and completion of that particular work. Saturn as timekeeper of what must be realized, practiced, and skillfully demonstrated in a consistent way helps us ground spiritual energy appropriate to our "true function," so we can master ourselves and see how to embody our life purpose.

This is why Saturn is associated with "destiny," and therefore the important choices we make that shape our character. "Character is destiny," since as we shape our character by our actions, feelings, and thoughts, we thereby shape our destiny. As we respond to the karmic effects of prior causes, and choose our responses to the mass of future potentials and outcomes, we reveal the ability to adapt or stay stuck in prior patterns. As we learn to examine anxieties, apprehensions, and assumptions objectively, we find a greater range of possible approaches to the challenges which will make us greater than our fear, sense of "not knowing," and powerlessness in the face of needed decisions.

Because Saturn is related to how we shape our destiny, it clearly is associated with karma. It brings the results of how we have acted and leads to the hard realization there is no avoiding the lessons resulting from prior choices shaping our karma. Saturn shows us consequences, and those obligations and duties which must be fulfilled, or confronted in a different form at each new turn of the karmic wheel. I'll discuss more about Saturn's function as the "keeper of karmic tally" in the next chapter.

SATURN - TAKING COMMAND OF OUR FATE

Saturn measures our ability to respond to circumstances, but sometimes this means action, and other times non-action. Sometimes we need more patience with the process, while at other times we must quicken our resolve and apply Saturn's quality of "enlightened self-interest," finding a newer, more appropriate set of responsibilities and interests to fulfill.

While Saturn sometimes brings a sense of heaviness and seriousness to all it touches, it also brings wisdom learned over time and experience, and a sense of how we might accomplish what we feel we need to in various life areas over time. Saturn teaches us how temporary limitations are the playground where we can know how to use time and discipline to accomplish what we need to at each stage of creating our life.

Later in the book I'll speak about various types of Saturn transits and how they affect us, how we can use them to best effect, and how they fit into the larger narrative of our Divine Path to self-mastery and Self-realization. Saturn teaches us that it takes time and structure to achieve a higher, greater destiny. No one ever lived their higher destiny without a well formed sense of who they were and who they weren't. No one ever became a Master of the Wisdom if they could be thrown off their equilibrium in deleterious ways by external things. Mastering Saturn's virtues ensures this can never happen again, since as we embrace those virtues, we become the Masters of our lives, and therefore the types of karmas we generate and leave behind.

Saturn shows us just how much control we have over "fate" or "destiny." Through Saturn related experiences we are shown whether we're referencing the lower ego or the Higher Ego. The more serious the challenge, the more the lower ego will feel threatened, and the more the Higher Ego will accept it as an opportunity to "break on through to the other side." Ultimately, the Higher

Ego serves the Soul, whereas the lower ego serves the separated self that dies at our last breath.

Over time, Saturn demonstrates everything serving the separated self, the self-grasping and self-cherishing mind, is an illusion, chased by the illusion of the mind seeking recognition and a sense of permanence. However, the fear-based ego-mind is doomed to a million apparent failures, since there is no permanence in anything the lower ego finds and attempts to hold on to.

The lower ego always chases chimera. It is in its nature, and why the lower mind is inherently pessimistic. It endlessly searches for knowledge, but never really "knows." It processes endless information but never comes to finality of "knowing" anything outside of its sequence and selection process.

Only the heart truly knows, and the heart is ruled by the Sun. As noted earlier, a healthy Sun externalizes through a healthy Saturn, and a healthy Saturn externalizes through a healthy Sun. Each serves the other in showing us the Light of our personal solar system as well as the boundaries of that system within which Life unfolds in perfect harmony with the Divine order.

Saturn helps us understand how to use time wisely as we master each step on our path to wisdom. Saturn also teaches us not to push our realizations and methods on those who are not mature enough to value what we have to offer. When it's time to be loving, then we can be the love we need to be. When it's time to be patient, then we will naturally choose patience over impatience. When it's time to defer gratification, then we won't fall into unhelpful states of wishing for more here and now. Through Saturn, we learn to leave behind unhelpful responses which could make things worse rather than better.

Saturn's energy rightly applied offers us the maturity and experience to steer the ship of our life purpose to its highest manifestation. Alternatively, Saturn's rigidity and inertia can keep us trapped by fear, obsolete rules and/or obligations deadening our life force. Either we

♄ Saturn: Spiritual Master, Spiritual Friend

choose appropriate and effective disciplines and grow into an ever-more perfect manifestation of our Dharma, our highest and truest purpose for being alive on Earth, or we choose to feed on "crushed stone" dominating the landscape which deadens our lives. We'll explore how Saturn relates to Dharma in Chapter Four.

Because it is also associated with the all-important universal binding force called the "Ring Pass Not," Saturn marks the limits of what we can achieve until we master all within that specific boundary. It is the far edge of our life and awareness where the known meets the unknown, and expands as our awareness expands. Saturn makes it clear over time that each step secured becomes the foundation for the next step to be taken. Saturn skips nothing, overleaps nothing, takes account of everything, proceeds of its own necessity, and doesn't move one bit faster or slower than it will, regardless of externals. We'll explore more about the mysterious thing known as the "Ring Pass Not" in Chapter Five.

TRANSITING SATURN HELPS US RESTRUCTURE OUR SENSE OF SELF

Saturn's movement is slower than all the other visible planets. Our inner Saturn teaches us how to master every detail of every lesson. We cannot know who we really are, and what greater roles we are to play on the stage of Life, until Saturn completes an entire 29 year cycle. And since life is a continuum, after that we embark on yet another 29 year journey of discovering more about our true Self based in the truths we've learned and the maturity we've demonstrated in the earlier cycle. Later on we'll explore the 29 year "whole cycle" and "the Saturn Return" and explore the freedom it promises those who accept the understanding it brings.

The house Saturn transits indicates the life area where we're learning to use Saturn's energies to

Saturn: Spiritual Master, Spiritual Friend

restructure our understanding of the affairs associated with that house. When Saturn moves through a house in our chart, those life affairs become a focus where we can find a greater sense of security by choosing what to hold on to and what to leave behind. And, just as Saturn shows a time of restructuring of the life areas associated with the houses it transits, it also works the same way each time Saturn touches the various planets in our charts.

As we discussed in the last chapter, the houses show us the various departments of our outer life and affairs and the planets show us our "inner Lights" which shine through the filters of the signs. These are the components of personality we are learning to master so we can have perfect self-expression according to our essential nature. When Saturn conjuncts our planets we are given an opportunity to restructure those planetary functions, making them more mature, organized, and effective in their expression. We'll explore many types of Saturn transits in the second half of this work.

As soon as transiting Saturn enters any sign, we all get advance signals about Saturn's future influence on any planet we have in that sign, even if the planet is at the end of the sign. Remember, too, Saturn in any given sign impacts billions of people, but in different ways based in their individual conditions. Saturn allows each of us to restructure what we need to, each in our own way, as we come to a more patient understanding of our destiny.

Our evolution is an unbroken continuum of awakening to a larger understanding of the interrelationships between All-That-Is and our unique function and part to play within that all-encompassing Oneness of Life. Due to the nature of the process, with each new level of self-awareness, many things are drawn together in newer, vaster perspectives of the relationship of the lower self to the Higher Self. With each lesson of spiritual maturity realized and demonstrated, we come to see how many prior skills and potentials present themselves in familiar but new ways.

♄ Saturn: Spiritual Master, Spiritual Friend

What is truly essential to our evolution can never be lost, since those skills, gifts, and specialized qualities will inevitably be resurrected for new times as new needs arise. We may not be doing the same things in the same way, but we will be doing a new "synthesis of Self" in new circumstances providing the proving grounds for a higher expression of Self.

With each turn of the wheel of our eternal Self-creation, we find both familiar and unfamiliar patterns. Evolution is a spiral, where we move in repetitive patterns showing us what we have mastered, and what we have yet to master, but always from a different perspective as a function of time and experience.

Saturn's influence is slow, steady, inexorable, and doesn't yield an inch of understanding we haven't won honestly. When transiting Saturn visits a significant point in our chart, things often feel heavier and slower, accompanied with a sense of finality. However, through maturity and experience we learn to adjust to the rhythm of what is, and become clear about what we can no longer hold on to, and what we must accept.

Saturn is the Timekeeper in the Game of Life, and the Guardian of Boundaries as we quest for Truth. It shows us how to take things one step at a time, as well as when it's appropriate to "trim the deadwood from our Tree of Life." Saturn teaches us how to act to make our lives and consciousness lighter. It helps us close old ways of feeling, thinking, relating, and efforting, while opening us to newer, more solid and reliable ways of living these qualities.

While life endings often feel like they're happening too fast, in fact every ending of every life chapter is prepared well in advance, and happens precisely when it should, as long as our resistance and/or need to control outcomes isn't postponing the process. Even then, at some point we still learn to let go. When we accept the finality of certain life experiences, we can find we've been simultaneously restructuring other parts of our life and have gone through a new set of experiences that have prepared us for a journey into greater understanding than

♄ Saturn: Spiritual Master, Spiritual Friend

we've ever imagined. If we hang in there long enough, and take the time to gain wisdom from our experiences, we can find an understanding of the value of every Saturn virtue, and ride the waves of life with grace, acceptance, and wisdom.

♄ Saturn: Spiritual Master, Spiritual Friend

CHAPTER 4
SATURN, DHARMA, AND KARMA

The birth chart shows our pure potential, and how each part of our inner makeup relates to all the other parts of our inner makeup, offering us ten thousand possible ways to fulfill our potential. However, because of the values of our cultural and family matrix, these can only be worked out initially through the natal environment.

As much as we may be "free" to express ourselves as children, we are still confined within the safety of the family and cultural matrix. To step outside of the boundaries, superstitions, and assumptions of the matrix before we're ready to fly on our own usually brings opprobrium, criticism, scorn, or some other punishment demonstrating the boundaries of where we can go and where we cannot.

Childhood is the period when we constantly push the outer limits of our ability to expand our scope of skill and awareness. As a result of childhood and family cultural assumptions that form us, over time we are led to different types of crises symbolized by the planets. Through the various challenges to our assumptions about how we should express ourselves, we find that we and others and everything else in our life wave must grow beyond familiar comfort zones.

When we are still children and the various parts of our personality are being formed, our freedom is really only

♄ Saturn: Spiritual Master, Spiritual Friend

a freedom to experiment within relatively secure test conditions predetermined by forces beyond our control. However, within those conditions we are able to catch glimpses of our true Self, and where we fit in (or don't) within the collective field of our childhood associations and beliefs.

Crises of growth inevitably are a result of choosing different ways of responding outside of the "group think" or "consensus reality" of those we're raised with, as well as later on when we are confronted with the need to hew our own course regardless of the approval or disapproval of our peers and teachers. This often means breaking with traditional beliefs and responses which those around us may take for granted.

When a crisis is precipitated in our lives, regardless of which planets are involved, we confront the need to go through a personal transformation. A crisis usually occurs when we are trying to live an old way that no longer feeds our evolutionary potential, and receive a clear signal that we must grow in a different direction, or re-commit to our life focus with a greater striving and determination. From one point of view, all crises come from our "true Self" hitting a limit where we confront something requiring our ego's attention and skill in dealing with it.

FULFILLING AND TRANSCENDING THE FAMILY AND CULTURAL MATRIX

From the moment we are born, we are how our planets express, how they grow, and how they exemplify the interactive physical, emotional, mental, and spiritual complex of our holographic existence. Our growth involves a mix of both familiar and unfamiliar experiences, some of which test our assumptions, beliefs, and conditioning.

Our level of awareness allows us to know how and why we come to the challenges we do. Each time we realize some assumptions must be changed, it results in

88

♄ Saturn: Spiritual Master, Spiritual Friend

natural evolutionary leaps. As we go through changes, we will feel the "fire by friction" as we leave old ways behind. Because each choice we make in our quest for greater understanding generates increasing distinctions between old views and a new awareness, at key points in the evolutionary process we encounter various kinds of crises.

Ego challenges are inevitable as a function of the evolutionary process. A crisis is a time to look at how an old ego expression of one or more planetary functions has become inadequate in some way, and find a better way to express our strengths effectively. Those who try to avoid their need to evolve do so at their own peril, since it generates more challenges, because the entire universe works as one force to help us to perfect our personality expression.

We become spiritual adults through facing crises directly (Saturn), with openness to what we are to learn and demonstrate to resolve those crises and come to a greater sense of our freedom (Uranus). Regardless of the nature of the crisis, we have the freedom to choose whether to face all of it, or part of it, or none of it, but because all crises came about as a result of our own evolving consciousness, if we don't deal with them at one time, we will have to deal with them at another. This is where Saturn and Uranus work together over time to assist us to individualize.

When we are young children, we take it for granted we must model the behavior and protocols of the adults around us. This is a function of the Moon, the means by which we adapt and mirror the authorities in our life during childhood. Our early years are a time when we begin to manufacture an ego structure arising from the desire for a sense of solidity and relative comfort so we can interact with others as equals rather than as supplicants looking for parental or societal permission before we choose courses of action. We all want to feel safe expressing ourselves in the world. That's why we choose to emulate certain values which permit us to grow in the relative safety of the family and cultural matrix.

♄ Saturn: Spiritual Master, Spiritual Friend

When we are younger and developing the lower ego, of necessity we use the tools and values we've learned from the cultural matrix. Our pre-formed ego is not really who we are; it is a manufactured entity and a temporary place holder until we find ways to enhance its power, or transcend it entirely. It is a construct that helps us deal with the pressures of the social environment, and the accumulation of learned responses to social and cultural demands on our evolving awareness. Some of them are consciously chosen, while others are unconscious patterns we've built into our mental and emotional vehicles for coping purposes.

When we become teens and young adults, we still are heavily under the influence of cultural norms, and try to define who we are within those norms, even as we seek experiences outside of those known values. Because it is in the nature of all things to grow beyond familiar references, over time we find ourselves confronting situations where we either reaffirm learned values and responses, or rebel against them because they are inadequate to explain or deal with the crises we confront. The key to mastering evolution is to learn to be ever-more conscious in the choices we make and why we are making them. Are we trying to conform to a set of inadequate or unfulfilling behaviors? Are we trying to fit the unknown into the known? Are we trying to use the skills of a child to deal with the crises of our adult life?

Saturn helps us understand the limitations of our religion, belief systems, and social-cultural matrix as we deal with life experiences pushing our personality growth. While our childhood conditioning and early adult assumptions are necessary up to a point, because of our eternal nature, the evolutionary process leads always to crises of individualization. These crises challenge us to learn and/or bring forth skills helping us transcend conscious and unconscious patterns which create trouble, problematic emotional responses, and any sense of incompetence as we deal with precipitated the crises to begin with.

♄ Saturn: Spiritual Master, Spiritual Friend

All crises serve to make us more aware of self-perpetuating negative influences we must transcend. As we become more aware, and choose to transmute negative and ineffectual responses into positive and more effective responses, we individualize as Soul/Spirits who can cultivate and maintain good human relationships as well as healthy attitudes about who we are, who we're not, and what we're here to do and be. Then we've effectively transcended any sense of helplessness when confronted with a crisis, since we have the power to choose how we want to navigate it, unhindered by family, religious, or cultural limitations.

SATURN, DHARMA, DESTINY, AND OUR TRUTH OF BEING

The birth chart shows us what we were born with, what we must cultivate, and what we must deal with, because of who we are as an evolving consciousness learning to master our planetary expressions. With each stage of personal mastery we attain, Saturn offers clues to our life mystery by showing us the next step in our never ending path to personal perfection. Because it is the Dweller on the Threshold, as well as the Angel of the Presence, our inner Saturn keeps us firmly bound to our destiny, even as it never lets us forget we are learning how to be a living, loving Soul/Spirit in the world. As Guardian of the Gates of Gold, it is the unyielding and all-seeing gatekeeper we confront in order to renounce fear and all that keeps our Eternal Consciousness bound by the lower egoic chains of half-truths and perceptions.

As our spiritual gatekeeper, Saturn keeps us on task as we fulfill our Dharma, a Sanskrit term approximately meaning "true function," but it could as easily be said it is what we are "destined" to dare to BE. Dharma is who we are, apart from our ideas and feelings and tendencies accumulated across many lifetimes.

91

♄ Saturn: Spiritual Master, Spiritual Friend

Dharma is beyond any ability to describe it. It is both noun and verb, and infuses our entire evolutionary process. Dharma has many facets, and cannot be confined to any specific set of descriptors. It is equivalent to the Tao in Taoist philosophy. It has been said "the Tao that can be known is not the ultimate Tao." It is the same with Dharma.

While we can glimpse many elements of Dharma, it cannot be confined to any narrow set of functions, truths, or ways of evolving. It is your "Truth of Being," the authentic "You" that is who you ARE vibrating to the pulses of Life throughout your perceived existence.

Dharma shows you the recurring themes of your life which must be fulfilled by your own "God force," or Highest Self. You may sense Dharma in moments of profound silence, or in the midst of the cacophony of life. You may find it in moments of greatest intensity, or deepest peace.

Dharma is where all harmonized and conflicted parts of YOU come together in the fragmentation and wholeness indicated by your birth chart. Dharma resolves the contradictions, and over time presents you with the infinite variables of your Eternal Self as it experiments with expressing your "Truth of Being" through your five senses and your mind.

There is no fighting Dharma, or rejecting Dharma. It is beyond your ability to fight it or reject it, since the former will just exhaust you as you learn to surrender to Dharma, and the latter will inevitably lead you back to Dharma. Basically, even when we try to reject Dharma, if it really is our Dharma, we'll still wind up living it, whether our minds have accepted or rejected any part of it.

Dharma forces us to examine all prior values and behaviors to see what is true for us at each turn of life's wheel. Dharma compels us to accept the fact that everything we've ever learned and thought in our childhood and long wave evolutionary process is subject to review by our Higher Self. In this way we learn what we can hold as valuable once we've stepped outside of the limited family and cultural matrix we were raised within, and what must be rejected as not in line with our true Self.

♄ Saturn: Spiritual Master, Spiritual Friend

Dharma is always in accord with the Divine Order in our evolution, and those experiences by which we understand our "true" duties, conduct, virtues, and ways of living appropriate to our state of consciousness in every moment of existence. However, Dharma is also beyond these forms. Dharma always leads us to the path of "righteous function," and supports us even when we feel we've lost our way.

DHARMA IS UNIQUE TO EACH INDIVIDUAL

Each astrological chart reveals a unique picture of a unique Being with a unique destiny. Each has what is easy, and each has what is difficult. Everything has value when it comes to Dharma, since each astrological factor and each crisis faced during life offers us a potential to re-envision our place in the larger whole of Life within which we live and breathe and have our Being.

While crises are certainly not the only means to realize and fulfill Dharma, we often learn more through the spur of necessity than through comfortable conditions since it intensifies our striving. Our lives are a miracle of constant growth through an ever growing awareness of how to use both pleasurable and painful circumstances to come out of attachments, aversions, illusions, and pessimism. From one point of view, every life experience reveals whether we are identifying with our lower self or our Higher Self, and how well the lower and higher are integrated.

A human being is actually a "six-pointed Star hologram" grounding Spirit in matter in a fluid dynamic interlocking energy. We are all a combination of an "upper Triad" of our eternal Self blended and expressed through the "lower triad" of personality.

The upper Triad is known in the East as "Atma-Budhi-Manas," the non-dual eternal Soul/Spirit awareness we always are, have been, and will be. The lower Triad of

93

♄ Saturn: Spiritual Master, Spiritual Friend

body, feelings, and the rational mind are the vehicles to be disciplined and trained in order to express our eternal Self's purpose for being here on Earth.

Mastering the personality so it can be a perfect vehicle for expressing our eternal self requires experiences helping us learn to realize and live the all-important Love, Wisdom, and active Divine Intelligence which are our eternal nature. By learning to identify with these Divine qualities, we find ways to manage this marvelous, contrary, and occasionally rebellious vehicle involving the body, feelings, and mind, while also learning to have a sense of humor about the entire perfectly imperfect human experience.

Though we are all human Beings with an upper and lower triad, we come into personhood at the time shown by the birth chart. Even though we share our birth moment with countless others around the world, we also are unique, since no other has both the exact birth moment as we do with the same environmental, family, and cultural factors. This combination of nature and nurture allows each of us a unique Dharma which is ours alone.

As we fulfill Dharma, we will catch glimpses of how our Dharma shares similar elements, circumstances, and realizations as others we meet along the way. Some of these will correspond with various planetary lessons we've dealt with, or are dealing with. And yet no one in the world shares our exact Saturn positions and conditions. Even when there are close similarities, we each have made individual choices in different circumstances on our life paths.

Saturn guides us through various modes of training and teaches us we are the authors of our Divine destiny, showing the way to becoming the living Light that cannot be dimmed. Our inner Saturn holds the key to the perfection and completion of our personality integration so we can express our Higher Triad in ways that are perfect for the roles we are to play on Earth. That also gives Saturn an association with the higher Way we are called to

♄ Saturn: Spiritual Master, Spiritual Friend

fulfill after our Earth incarnations are finished. Of course, this is not limited to current life Saturn positions. As I offered earlier, Saturn binds time, yet is also beyond time. Even when we've mastered this four dimensional existence, there are still other realms to explore, greater awareness to experience, and a more powerful Love to BE.

HOW DHARMA RELATES TO OUR ETERNAL FREEDOM

Because each stage of life and evolution, once mastered, opens doors to a more advanced Life and evolution, it is easy to see that both Saturn and Uranus have associations with Dharma. Uranus symbolizes our eternal freedom to explore all there is in the eternity and infinity of existence. While Saturn binds us to certain lessons until we master them, Uranus always calls us to embrace the adventure of accepting complete autonomy and an ever expanding individuality.

Whereas Saturn shows us reality, Uranus offers us inspiration and flashes of genius. While Saturn binds us to the causes and effects related to destiny, Uranus offers us on-going individualizing experiences where we demonstrate our freedom to cut loose from those things which trap us in restrictive patterns inhibiting our growth. While Saturn binds us through fear of the unknown, Uranus throws us into the unknown NOW with every breath we take.

Saturn and Uranus represent the boundaries of our imagination and the gateway to creative individuality. When we learn to use these energies wisely, each in the right way and time, our potential is limitless, and each thing we master, acquired through practice and patience, becomes our individual path to freedom and higher purpose.

♄ Saturn: Spiritual Master, Spiritual Friend

Uranus awakens us to the power of creative imagination. Saturn helps us structure imagination into forms of creative visualization. We have the power of creative visualization any time we want to use it. In the quest to fulfill Dharma, we have to learn what to dream and how to dream with an eye to what can and cannot be accomplished of our own will.

Since Dharma rules all, we can learn a lot by examining where Spirit and Matter meet within us, the critical zone between our inspiration and the realities of life. This is where the eternal freedom of Uranus dances with the binding forms of Saturn we live within, until we cast off those old Saturn forms for newer forms that are adequate containers so our evolved Divine Self-expression can naturally come forth.

While we are Eternals having human experiences, not all human experiences are ours to own, since some are not appropriate to who we are and what we're here to learn. While we may embrace countless experiences, many of these have a very short time span as we walk our walk, since we evolve with every choice we make. What may be appropriate for a period of time when we're younger may not be allowed at all as we mature into greater spiritual awareness and purpose.

Uranus is the eternal spark of Divine individuality symbolizing revolutionary movements that we often do not comprehend. Saturn binds, while Uranus liberates. We have both forces working on us all the time, in both material and non-material ways, which is why we must become aware of they are manifesting in our lives. Too much Saturn can breed pessimism and an unhealthy sense of limitation, while too much Uranus sends our head spinning into furthest space disconnected from our body. An unhealthy Uranus will run us over a precipice, while an unhealthy Saturn keeps us in prisons of our own making.

Dealing with these two simultaneously occurring forces teaches us how to "make our freedom real," while living a constant revolution in how we view forms that temporarily bring us security. Uranus is ungrounded

Saturn: Spiritual Master, Spiritual Friend

inspired individual freedom eternally exploring infinite possibilities, while Saturn teaches us the limits of our ability to shape certain elements of our ex-pressed reality within the fourth dimensional field of time.

While we may want to believe all things are possible, in fact they may not be possible for us, and even when they are, their manifestation is bound within the field of time. Even if something is possible for us to manifest, each thing we experience in life has its time of appearance, its time of manifestation, and its time to end. Some things cannot be pushed into manifestation, since they have their own rhythm of existence apart from our sense of time as the creator. Each appearance has its appointed season, and each thing has its "pulse of creation."

In an example of one archetypal span of creation, it takes about nine months (if all goes well) for a pregnancy to produce a child. Over my years of practicing and teaching the science of thought form building and the art of crafting affirmations, I have observed it often does take about nine months for our labors and efforts to manifest as well, especially those things marking life altering creations and the events that inevitably follow in their train.

I have found some things can be created in a very short time; other creations take longer. Some creations require a little effort and some tending to their maturity; other creations require a lot of effort and a tremendous commitment through many trials, obstacles, and delays. Our attitude in large part determines what does or doesn't manifest, since attitude either supports the creation or frustrates it.

Not all labors come to a form of satisfactory fulfillment. Again, not all experiences are ours to have. The River of Life has its own tides and timing apart from the skill of those navigating those waters, and sometimes we are called to learn through apparent defeats rather than apparent victories. Though difficult, these experiences teach us valuable lessons and help us become more spiritually mature.

♄ Saturn: Spiritual Master, Spiritual Friend

Finding a healthy spiritual maturity involves learning how to blend our Saturn function with our Uranus function in a healthy balance, keeping us on track as we refine all of our other planetary expressions over time. There can be no enduring form without Saturn's firm and mature hand guiding the Spirit seeking eternal discovery. Inspiration is always there but it takes the structure of Saturn to make it manifest. Eventually, our freedom to know what to do and when will consistently bring us a sense of being at peace with who we are.

While we are free to explore infinite possibilities related to our path to Truth, we cannot experience what is not within our "Ring-Pass-Not," even though it holds an almost limitless set of experiences which offer us potential forms of enlightenment perfect for who we are. We cannot live any other Dharma than our own, but that Dharma is magnificent in its possible expressions on our never-ending journey of eternal awakening leading us and our world to an ever deeper and vaster awareness than we've known before.

As you continue to dream, consciously and unconsciously, your highest ideal life as you would like to see it made manifest in the future, remember you also want to open to innovative ways to create and shape your life so it's perfect for your future growth into your Higher Self. Again, a sense of humor and perspective is needed, since sometimes what is perfect for the growth of our Higher Self doesn't look very pleasing to the ego with its limited views.

That's why some degree of detachment, dispassion, and discrimination are useful as we create and then see the various pushes and pulls requiring us to re-evaluate and refine some things to alter the trajectory of our thought forms. It's also why cultivating the ability to turn the mind from its natural negativity toward a positivity is necessary. When one approach doesn't work, rather than default to negativity, we instead have the ability to point our minds toward more positive directions before the negativity arises.

98

♄ Saturn: Spiritual Master, Spiritual Friend

With practice, we will find we have the ability not to play to illusions, attachments, and aversions, since we'll have the power to change life patterns by being open to a higher, broader awareness of what is in our best interests. Regard the dreaming of how to create a better future life as an "experiment in Truth," and be willing to adjust what needs adjusting as you see your ideal made manifest over time. Our entire physical existence is a "thought experiment" by our eternal Self.

Combine the inventive inspiration of Uranus with the steady patient works of Saturn and enjoy your journey of Self-realization as you move through the changes associated with any creation. If you do what must be done in the right way and time, whatever you're attempting to dream into future reality will result in you living a different Truth and life appropriate to your evolving Higher Self. That will affect the rest of your life, so dream wisely, grasshopper!

KARMA MUST BE FULFILLED ON OUR ROAD
TO MASTERING WISDOM

Besides its association with Dharma, Saturn is also associated with Karma. While it is widely accepted that karma involves "cause and effect" patterns, Karma cannot be confined to such a narrow view. Not all "good karma" is the result of good actions in the past, and not all "bad karma" is the result of negative actions in the past. It's not that simple to know what caused various types of Karma, and why we confront them when we do. This is part of our Divine Mystery.

There are many kinds of Karma, though they all fall into one of two main groups. Knowing the differences in the types of Karma can explain why things happen as they do. I have termed them "Big K" Karma and "little k" karma. There is a huge difference between "Big K" Karma and

ℏ Saturn: Spiritual Master, Spiritual Friend

"little k" karma.

Both "Big K" and "little k" karmas arise from many complex factors in our existence. While they are somewhat interrelated, they are distinctly different types of Karma. The two types of karma arise from different causes, and are vastly different in how they work. We have far more power to create, uncreate, or change the second type than we do the first type.

BIG K KARMA AND SACRED WOUNDS

"Big K" Karma is built into our hologram at birth. These are primary causal energies we must understand as part of our journey to Self-realization. They include Sacred Wounds by which we are challenged to come to powerful forms of compassionate service for others who suffer the same challenges. They bring forth major lessons we must learn in order to move beyond being trapped by the limitations of the lower ego.

Every being has at least one of the Sacred Wounds. Some have more than one. Each one cuts us to the core, and by moving into the "underworld" associated with those sorts of Divine wounds and "coming back to life" in the appointed season, we learn how to contribute to the greater good in our world.

Sacred Wounds help us serve with authenticity, since no external thing can diminish or take away the primal power of these direct life-altering experiences. "Big K" Karmic events are often known as "Acts of God," or at the very least, "forces beyond our control." There are many things we confront in life that we didn't cause which alter our lives in profound ways, forever changing how we respond in the future.

While some Sacred Wounds happen only to adults, there are others which happen when we are children. Some are born with a Sacred Wound, while other Sacred Wounds happen as a function of our life and destiny. Then

100

ħ Saturn: Spiritual Master, Spiritual Friend

there are the life-altering wounds directly caused by the adults in our lives, whether deliberately or unconsciously.

We certainly can't assume young children directly cause the events that wound them, since they have no ability to influence whether an adult chooses to wound them or not. Childhood wounds are beyond our control, since through no action of our own, we were forced to confront life-altering events that shaped us in a primal way.

A few examples of sacred wounds are physical violation, abandonment, betrayal, and having too strict, confining, smothering, harsh or even brutal conditions in childhood. Obviously there are other archetypal wounds which could fall in the realm of a "Sacred Wound." Just as we are not apart from our planets, neither is our experience as we work it out through the people we journey with during each phase of life. When we are wounded in a life-altering way, there is usually a clear planetary signal being sent related to a facet of a deeper Sacred Wound, as well as the self-healing we need to do.

There are various types of biological wounds that exemplify the nature of a Sacred Wound. Since we are a hologram, a physical wound will always be associated with emotional and mental wounds, just as emotional and mental wounds caused by adults often result in self-destructive physical behaviors. An examination of the various planetary dysfunctions when taken to an archetypal level will reveal the basic sets of Sacred Wounds, as well as the antidotes to these wounds.

Because this is "Big K" Karma, there will always be a sense of being forced by circumstances to deal with what we must, and accepting some things are just the way they are. We may be fulfilling a certain Karma, whether our own or the Karma of another for some unknown reason. Time changes all things when it comes to the material creation. How much more so the emotional and mental creation, from which all material creations come from?

Any Sacred Wound, whether physical or psychological, creates profound and deep mental and emotional damage. Since they affect us in primary ways,

ħ Saturn: Spiritual Master, Spiritual Friend

there is never a time when we forget those primal wounds since they scar us to our core. They will surface in many ways throughout our lives, even when we are mature and may have practiced a spiritual discipline for years. We simply learn to deal with it, and continue to deal with those primal patterns throughout our lives, until we are fully realized beings. That is why our wounds are excellent for learning how to express a greater compassion for ourselves and all others who suffer.

All deep crippling wounds must be seen as spurs to our Soul, offering us opportunities to heal them through coming out of weakness, victimization, anger, and fear into strength, courage, connectedness, and love. Healing those life-altering, crippling wounds is not about forgetting them, since they've affected our lives forever. Still, we must break free of the heavy gravitational field of the memory of the experience associated with the wound which initially entrapped us.

Breaking free of the gravitational heaviness requires an unwavering courage, determination, and compassion when confronting the wound and repudiating its power to affect our life in deadening ways. For some, it means becoming a voice for all others who share that wound, while others choose to be the witness for all those who have suffered that wound, but don't have the voice or sense of mission to bring the issues of the wound into their world.

Even though Sacred Wounds seem to come from "forces beyond our control," by how we respond to the wound we generate future karmic patterns. By going to the depth of the wound and establishing contact with what we know will help us "get through the night" and eventually a measure of healing, we shape our Saturn expression and find an understanding of ourselves and others who share that wound.

One key to knowing we have learned what we needed to know is when we recognize, consciously in the here and now, that we are not at the mercy of our woundedness, and can act with a mature strength and

ℏ Saturn: Spiritual Master, Spiritual Friend

sensitivity rather than weakness and a sense of victimization. As we grow, we can put a lot of distance between any prior sense of helplessness or inability to act in effective and satisfying ways while discovering a wide smorgasbord of effective responses demonstrating our power to reject being spiritually debilitated by our wounds.

As spiritual adults, we can reflect on our deficiencies, go to the depth of them, laugh at them, and claim our power to transcend negative reactions those deficiencies once triggered in us. We can look with dispassion at those things which once made us afraid or paralyzed us, and generate a greater compassion for ourselves and suffering humanity. We then stand in the Light of Time as autonomous, conscious Soul/Spirits, unafraid of whatever we might confront, because we have taken charge of our responses and are free to be a Light in our world.

A major sign post on the healing journey leading us from darkness to light and from isolation to a sense of connection with others is when we understand we share archetypal wounds with countless others across space and time. In our shared woundedness and willingness to embrace the strength arising from consciously transmuting any sense of victimhood into courage, compassion, and conviction, we become a source of healing and validation of the power of Love to redeem the promise of a better life for those we meet who share those wounds.

Through healing our wounds and learning to live well despite them, we bring meaning and purpose out of these larger events, and become a living example of a higher Way. As we learn to cope with our debilities and find ways to live so they don't hinder us, we find we are connecting with others who are also wounded. Over time this offers us the ability to set aside harsh judgments, eliminate any sense of shame or blame, and overcome any feelings of isolation and separateness related to our evolutionary challenges.

As we embrace the process of healing our Sacred Wound(s), we learn to live what Rudhyar termed "the

Saturn: Spiritual Master, Spiritual Friend

symbolic life," and become a living exemplar of the power of Love expressed by the Light that shines through us as a result of healing our Sacred Wound. As we embrace the quest to heal our wounds, we learn how to transform the experience of those wounds, both large and small, into an ability to demonstrate a form of effective service in our world. Our wounds are the gateway to freedom. Our debilities show us the way to healing and power.

LITTLE K KARMA AND WHAT WE CAN DO ABOUT IT

We now turn to the other type of karma, which I have termed "little k" karma. We create these lesser karmas as we move through life experiences, which yield "good" or "bad" results based on our actions and inactions. They are important markers of patterns showing us ways to modify our behavior, feelings, and thoughts. Little "k" karmas are created through acts of omission or commission, and we learn to confront and resolve the consequences of those actions and non-actions by seeing how they came to be, and taking responsibility to change what needs changing.

Throughout childhood and early adult life, we had to respond the best we were able to challenging situations. Our actions and reactions to those early experiences created patterns which manifested in diverse ways after those experiences. They shaped our personality by setting up cause and effect cycles which played out long after those initial events.

Little k karma involves some form of a reaction for every action. Put another way, what goes around comes around. Through this type of cause and effect cycle we learn if we say hurtful things, others feel sad and experience suffering. If we create suffering, we see it in others, and if they say or do hurtful things to us, we suffer. Through these experiences, we choose to shut down and

104

℞ Saturn: Spiritual Master, Spiritual Friend

become numb, or open to a greater mindfulness in our words and deeds, and examine what we want to give to others and receive from them.

"Little k" karmas are entirely the product of actions, thoughts, and feelings, and can be changed by altering behavior patterns. These types of karma are related to past responses conditioning future situations. Sometimes they manifest through others, and give us opportunities to change the cycles of cause and effect, whether in our lives or the lives of others.

That's not to say all misdeeds can be fixed, since as a great Persian philosopher once wrote, "the moving finger writes; and having writ, moves on; nor all your piety nor wit shall lure it back to cancel half a line, nor all your tears wash out a word of it." Even when we change our responses, it does not mean the past is undone. It merely means we are not perpetuating the pattern of acting, feeling, or thinking which resulted in those forms of karmic effects. We write the Book of Life with each response we make.

Sometimes when a "little k" karma has been fulfilled, and the tendency to act out an old pattern has been changed at the core and will not return, we confront the fact that the only thing left is to move on if there are no satisfactory amends to be made. These are times when a life chapter has closed, and there's nothing left to do but walk on and "sin no more," as we were once told by a Spiritual Master.

FAMILY KARMA

Family karma involves a combination of both Big K Karma and little k karma. I have heard some say they believe the family we are born into governs our Karma, and our parents' karma (both Big K and little k) influences the life we must live. While we are influenced to some degree by the karmas generated by our parents, ultimately we still

℞ Saturn: Spiritual Master, Spiritual Friend

have our own karmas, and they have their own karmas.

The choices our parents make influence our lives, but only up to a point. When our lower ego begins to take shape through our mind's sequence and selection process, we find we rely on some of those family and cultural patterns, but also separate from some of them.

As we individualize, we understand how we were conditioned by the family and cultural matrix of beliefs, superstitions, taboos, and aspirations, and can consciously choose to renounce and grow beyond those which are no longer adequate to our evolving higher awareness. Put another way, many family systems were fine for who we were when we were born, but are not appropriate for the Higher Self we are to become.

There is a widespread belief that often one or more family members are part of our larger "group Soul," and we are bound to the Karma generated by our group Soul. However, this illusion still places the power of how we evolve with external factors, when in truth our evolution is entirely determined by the interactions between our lower ego and Higher Self.

Whatever Karmas we deal with as part of a group Soul, even those we share with others in our family, in the final analysis we each have our own karmic path and lessons. It is impossible for any of us to live a previous generation's Karma, or anyone else's karma, since each of us has our own ticket to ride as we navigate the River of Life.

We all are born with a unique "vintage" within a larger "vintage" of the times. Each generation must deal with the issues and detritus of the previous generation, as well as the aspirations, illusions, and qualities of their own. There is also the all-important factor that life is a continuum that flows ever onward, and as we are constantly learning from and reacting to our past experiences, we also are forever compelled to deal with unforeseen and unintended developments in the here and now.

106

♄ Saturn: Spiritual Master, Spiritual Friend

In general, Pluto's sign positions show us the differences between generations. Because of the relationship of the signs to the ones preceding them and following them, each Plutonic generation represents what the previous generation seeks to draw on and make substantial, and each subsequent generation can learn from the "self-undoing" behaviors and motives of the traits of the previous generation.

In an astrological birth chart, because of the houses associated with parents and grandparents, there is often a fundamental friction between adjacent generations, while there is often an instinctive understanding across skipped generations. Many people can get along better with their grandparents than their parents, and their grandchildren get along better with them than their parents.

In Chapter Ten we'll go into greater depth about Pluto, and how Saturn crystallizes that Divine Power every 29 years. We'll take a look at Pluto's profound influence for all generations on Earth, and the times in the present and future when Saturn touched or will touch the "Lord of the Underworld" in everyone's existence.

KARMIC STORMS

In life there are three types of "karmic storms" that affect us personally. There are storms we created, or must confront resulting from our evolutionary process; there are storms created by others, which we may or may not have an ability to influence; then there are the karmic storms that are pandemic, affecting everyone in diverse ways.

The first type of karmic storm is associated with our birth chart, and the crises precipitated by progressed and transiting aspects to planets in the birth chart. The second type of karmic storm is related to the birth charts of others in our lives, while the third type of karmic storm can be seen by the aspects transiting planets make with each other in the real-time here and now affecting everyone in their own way. Often karmic storm zones are indicated by the square or opposition aspects, as they challenge "right action" involving the signs these aspects trigger, showing the forces in dynamic tension demanding managed release and expression.

In the first type of "karmic storm," we are put in the position of learning and doing what we must to resolve old karma, as well as prevent the continuance of unfortunate or unnecessary karmic patterns into the future. Our responses in these challenging periods help us to fulfill and complete old cause-and-effect cycles. However, if we try to ignore the lessons, the old patterns will continue until we choose to change them.

Basically, when we hit a personal "karmic storm," we either resolve the energetics, or perpetuate them into future cycles. Regardless of appearances or "fault," it is useless to blame our circumstances on others, since it's a transit or progression in our chart that brought the circumstance into our field of perception. When we learn the lesson, we won't have to go through such things again, though eventually we may be put in a position to help another deal with a similar situation or lesson. This brings us to the second type of karmic storm.

In the second kind of karmic storm, involving difficulties others are going through, we are put in the position of either being able to help them, or at least be a witness to what's going on. Then we have the lesson of learning or demonstrating discrimination and detachment so we don't accept another person's challenges, difficulties, lessons, or limitations as our own. It may also involve the need to learn how not to be attached to "helping" in ways that we take on someone else's baggage.

If we have gone through something that seems similar, then if it's appropriate we can suggest options. Either they accept our suggestions or not. As we navigate this second type of karmic storm zone, often the best way for us to serve the crisis is by being intensely positive and supportive of their higher intention. Even if they don't see it or comprehend it, we can affect the situation as positively

♄ Saturn: Spiritual Master, Spiritual Friend

as possible through this approach in another's moment of crisis.

The third type of "karmic storm" usually affects us in profound ways, since when we look to others we see they are having as hard a time as we are. Often there is confusion, no one seems to have solid answers to what's going on, and life seems more difficult than usual. In these periods much can seem muddled or unclear.

During karmic storm zones if we can open to the appropriate point of view and take none of it personally we can become a strength and laser-light beam to others who are lost in the storm. I believe if we open to being in harmony with whatever is needed in the moment, we become the embodiment of "the corrective force of Nature."

There is no karmic storm we confront, individually or collectively, that we cannot transcend, rising above the suffering while staying connected to the heart of compassion. There is no seeming impossibility where we cannot find a lovingly wise way to deal with it. There are no circumstances that can force us to yield to despair, discouragement, or the illusion of powerlessness. This is our true power, where we learn to bring forth the most positive response we can.

Regardless of what confronts us, if we find a productive way to approach a problematic collective atmosphere, we can help others find a way out of the confusion of wondering why this has come upon them or all of us. There may or may not be a "reason," but every circumstance allows us to act, feel, think, speak and become our Higher Self rather than yield to impotence or helplessness.

We do not have to participate in the generic suffering. We just need to keep our heads when others are losing theirs. And keep a sense of humor as we dance with the Divine play, remembering we are Eternals having human experiences.

♄ Saturn: Spiritual Master, Spiritual Friend

HOW MUCH CONTROL DO WE ACTUALLY HAVE?

I have heard it said that because something involves karma, we have little or no control over what manifests or not. This of course is an illusion. While we cannot do much about causes set into motion in the past, whether by ours or another's actions or inactions, or merely by circumstances, we can always transmute the energies in the NOW through "right realization" wisely applied.

All of us are accountable for our thoughts, words, and deeds. It's how we simultaneously work through and create karmas. When we're faced with a challenge, we can stop unfortunate tendencies which will create negative results in the future, and replace them with constructive responses which will generate beneficial effects. Remembering we are creating future karmic patterns by current choices, actions, feelings, and thoughts in any given moment can give us insights into our power to fulfill old karma and generate a newer, more positive future in the here and now.

Each one of us has our unique times and forms of fulfillment, rewards, and blessings, so it's folly to compare our process to anyone else's. If we rise to the challenge of individualization revealed in every crisis, we stop suffering over things being fair or unfair, and use the time to adjust our rules, assumptions, and sense of duty. Every crisis gives us an opportunity to let go of every corrosive or coercive thing in our past still affecting us in the present.

When old security systems are breaking down, dissolving, or getting annihilated, it's time to be flexible and balanced as we move through temporary "containers of personality" until the storm passes. Also remember that the forces of Karma don't necessarily work according to the same timeline we do, but they are unerring in discharging their function at exactly the right time and way according to how the karma was fixed to begin with.

For those who accept the reality of reincarnation, it

110

♄ Saturn: Spiritual Master, Spiritual Friend

helps to remember we created our patterns for this life by what we did and did not cultivate in prior incarnations, along with what we learned when we were in "the Heaven World," or Devachan. Since we cannot master everything in our evolution in any one, two, or even five lifetimes, we cannot afford to judge our karmic lessons or evolutionary process using our limited dualistic mind, since at best this generates a limited dualistic understanding. However, we can always access our Highest Self, which is non-dual. Our Highest Self exists on its own level, and eternally realizes countless ways it embodies love, wisdom, and our unique way of perfectly expressing our "Truth of Being" across countless lifetimes.

Since evolution is endless, and our lives are like ropes woven of Divine Threads, we'll never stop moving through experiences and gleaning wisdom from them. Both "Big K" Karma and "little k" karma serve to show us what is true and what is not true in our evolution from the unreal to the real, from darkness to light, and from death to immortality.

An important factor in our evolutionary journey is that from time to time our little k karma sets larger karmic patterns into motion leading us to the threshold of life changing transformations. Those are the times when our personality makes some seemingly minor choices that open major doors to a higher destiny through both pleasurable and painful experiences. This is when "little k" karma leads us directly to "Big K" Karma and the fulfillment of Dharma.

Various karmas play a part in how and when old duties and limitations close, and when new ones present themselves. We have some ability to speed up the karmic process by our willingness to do whatever it takes to examine why things are as they are, and how the past served as the source for the present. As we see our lives and evolution as a continuum, we can get glimpses of the many facets and manifestations of Dharma, and how our "Ring-Pass-Not" evolved as we did.

As I introduced in the last chapter, Saturn is

111

ℏ Saturn: Spiritual Master, Spiritual Friend

associated with the mysterious thing called "the Ring-Pass-Not." It defines the limits of what we must deal with before we can move into a greater life. The Ring-Pass-Not is unyielding when it comes to life karmas which must be fulfilled. However, once certain karmic patterns are fulfilled and viewed in the light of a greater understanding and wisdom, we can choose to say goodbye to old personality actions, feelings, and thoughts, and live more evolved ones which will allow us to fulfill our Soul's purpose in the future.

REFLECTION ON OUR WOUNDS

Since it's good to reflect on how some of the concepts we've discussed have played out in our lives, here are a few questions to ask yourself.

1. What are the most painful wounds you have experienced this lifetime? Did these originate in childhood, or come forth when you were an adult?
2. How did you deal with them at the time? How has your response to those wounds evolved over time?
3. In what ways did you replace a sense of powerlessness and victimization with a broader and deeper awareness of how to respond with clarity and focus, rather than confusion and uncertainty?
4. What life-long understanding about yourself came from those wounds? How did you evolve through learning how to deal with them?
5. How have you lived your life differently from those times in your life, and how have those wounds made you a better person?
6. What realizations have you come to as a result of meeting others who share your wound?

112

CHAPTER 5
SATURN
GUARDIAN OF THE RING-PASS-NOT

As Eternals learning how to be our true Self in the infinity of experience, this world provides us a great classroom so we can learn all we need to learn in this incarnation. However, there are stages to how our human self acquires knowledge and understanding. For example, we wouldn't expect a first grader to be able to absorb the principles of higher mathematics, but we can expect them to master addition and subtraction, and perhaps even multiplication depending on their aptitude.

This continues into adulthood. We have to learn to master a multitude of basic principles of action, feeling, thought, and aspiration before we're fit to learn and practice certain spiritual skills which allow us to take on effective roles in the world. Once we learn skills and practice roles where we are tested to apply our realizations and spiritual strengths, then we are able to further higher values, culture, and even the evolutionary process according to our Dharma.

As with any form of learning, it helps if there is an organized, coherent curriculum. Our Saturn function allows us to craft the forms we need to express the transpersonal ideals represented by the invisible outer quartet of Uranus, Neptune, Pluto, and TransPluto. It gives structure to how

ꝑ Saturn: Spiritual Master, Spiritual Friend

we interpret and express spiritual forces we're aligned with. Saturn represents how we consistently and persistently learn to be authors of our spiritual Self through binding our realizations as a function of time.

Life is a series of endless realizations. Realizations are the playground of the mind's love of discovering new information. However, there often seems to be more than one hang-up in how to apply those realizations in satisfactory ways. That's why we can have great realizations only to confront the mystery of not knowing what to do with them.

Our lives are stuffed to capacity with realizations we often do not know how to apply in satisfactory ways which can be the source of a lot of human frustration. When we have realized something but are unable to translate it into some form of action, the subconscious mind gets frustrated. We know what we know, but often become dissatisfied because we don't know how to apply the knowledge effectively. Still, as we learn to apply our realizations, without the ego-mind's fear of failure, harsh judgments, or procrastination intruding to mess things up, eventually through practice we begin to get a sense of competency in that area of life, and find skills perfectly suited to express our Dharma.

THE VALUE OF LIMITATIONS

All human beings are limited by circumstances, and most of us at one time or another have wondered why things are the way they are. Every person wants to break free of their limitations and overcome their blind spots. So why are we bound in time? Why must we endure certain limitations until we don't? Why are we limited by what we can and cannot do? What holds us back until it's time to move forward?

We all have the power to grow beyond limitations. They only oppress us until we learn our power to step

114

♄ Saturn: Spiritual Master, Spiritual Friend

outside of obsolete views into newer, healthier roles to play. As we learn not to take certain lessons personally, seeing through the lower ego perceptual traps, we can examine how we all have been limited by various aspects of our understanding which set up certain lessons, both individual and interactive, unique as well as recurring.

We must master certain approaches before seeking other fields of exploration, realization, application, and expertise. Limits are the means by which our quest for Truth becomes coherent. Sometimes they make sense to us, and other times they seem meaningless, frustrating, and heavier than iron chains.

Along the way we find we must confront the need to be realistic about our abilities, whether we're dealing with the limitations of outer forms or the inner limits of our lack of knowing how to respond to something. Through understanding the limitations we confront the value of accepting some (at least for a while) and learning how to overcome others, we are shown the coherency of our journey from incompetence to effectiveness.

Without Saturn we'd be adrift in an infinite sea of lessons, with no beginning, no end, no form, and no structure. Saturn represents the outer limits of what we're able to deal with in the moment. Everything that hinders us originated somewhere, since none of us is a victim of random circumstances. So just how and why do our limitations come to be?

As Soul/Spirits in the material world, we find a sense of significance and purpose by accepting certain voluntary limitations in order to focus our lives and intention in meaningful ways. Saturn represents "the limitations ordained by duty" we must accept if we are to fulfill our understanding of any given life experience and how it fits into our evolution from ignorance to higher awareness.

While there is no limit to the growth of the Soul, many different limitations of form shape different seasons of life. Through this we come to a well-rounded Wisdom, and are offered textures in our understanding through

115

♄ Saturn: Spiritual Master, Spiritual Friend

knowing when to stop, when to go, when to work, and when to play, across the physical, emotional, mental, or spiritual realms of experience.

It has been said some limits are necessary in the human condition, or we'd have no sense of direction for any length of time, since it is the nature of our Eternal Self to want to explore everything that comes across its perceptual field. Each of us is searching for a sense of significance and purpose in a world of seemingly endless possibilities. As free spirits, we get to choose the limits we will live with, until it's time to fulfill a greater purpose.

Saturn in its role as the "Ring-Pass-Not" prevents us from avoiding certain key lessons and responsibilities directly related to Dharma. As a result we learn the usefulness of reasonable limits, as well as when we can expand beyond them into broader realms and more appropriate ways of living. As we fulfill each step on the path to ever-greater awareness, it frees us to move on to new experiences. There are certain lessons we must master if we would grow beyond the fears and illusions that bind us.

While it is natural to feel hassled by some obligations and limitations, especially when we would rather be doing something else or experiencing a greater sense of freedom, they are absolutely necessary, since they show us what we are learning about how to maneuver within them to express our Higher Self in effective ways, now and in the future. Through understanding what limits us and what frees us, we learn about our evolutionary road map and the "rules of the road."

Many times in life it seems as though we're caught in "holding patterns," practicing skills and coming to realizations about things which may seem meaningless or futile in the moment. However, these set the stage for abilities we'll demonstrate in future life experiences and chapters. Some limits are more boon than burden, when seen from a larger angle of growth and development. The Ring-Pass-Not keeps us from those experiences we are not prepared for, and allows us to become familiar with

℟ Saturn: Spiritual Master, Spiritual Friend

what we have mastered while providing glimpses of what we have yet to master. As we understand what we need to, doors of perception open that were previously closed, and we can rest easy as we slowly and surely achieve forms of mastery allowing our Higher Self future opportunities to demonstrate what we've mastered in the Game of Life.

NAVIGATING DISILLUSIONMENT

What we clutch at and what we avoid are factors in how our Ring-Pass-Not is shaped at any given point in our evolution. So are the various illusions we encounter in learning how the five senses and the mind operate. Since illusions are everywhere, part of the path to personal mastery involves learning how to navigate occasional "disillusionment."

Because we are interactive beings, it is natural for our mind and feelings to fall prey to attachments, aversions, our own and others' illusions and delusions, suppositions, superstitions, and unreliable perceptions. It is why our evolutionary path requires us to learn how to recognize them, and overcome any tendency to fall into the mental traps created by these things. We define the field of our "dis-illusionment" through our predisposing patterns of attachments to perceptions and interpretations about life. Everything subject to our perceptions and interpretations becomes a temporary form we can learn from, both by its appearance and its eventual disappearance. How much fear, oppression, and sense of victimization or disempowerment we experience around the comings and goings of phenomena in life shows us facets of the Ring-Pass-Not.

Glamor often plays a big part in how we unnecessarily limit our possibilities, since glamor distracts us from the real. Glamor is fundamentally unreal and widely known as a world problem. However, at times it is a useful tool helping us to come out of delusions we may

♄ Saturn: Spiritual Master, Spiritual Friend

have about the nature of the lower self and its relationship to the Higher Self. Glamor also reveals our attachment to perceptions, as well as our relationship to Truth and Community.

Through the inevitable contrasts we perceive in the endless but necessary polarizations between the worlds of Spirit, Soul, and matter, we learn to master moving through duality. Through polarizations, we learn how to antidote doubts, illusions, superstitions, and other mental traps resulting from ego assumptions, as well as the mind's natural pessimism of suffering over its own suffering. All of these must be confronted and transmuted if we are to achieve relative forms of mastery and experience the expansion of the Ring-Pass-Not. Polarizations help us refine the "compare and contrast" function of the mind, and through cultivating Divine Discernment, we come to know the real as well as the unreal. Since illusions are unreal, it's better to be "disillusioned" than illusioned. With Saturn as our guide and friend, disillusionment can lead us to clarity, sanity, and the ability to express our Highest Self regardless of external factors.

FEAR IS A DANGEROUS DISEASE

Of all the traps we encounter on the way from darkness to Light, there is one more dangerous than any other, and that is fear. It is a crippling, destructive emotional virus keeping us afraid of all that threatens or is outside the conception of our lower ego. Since we are learning to be more conscious of our power to turn our mind toward beneficial things, then in the journey to higher awareness, this disease has no purpose except to show us the way beyond being affected by it.

Fear is pandemic. It pervades the collective consciousness. If we have any spiritual sensitivity at all, we will at times feel fear in others around us, even if we are not personally afraid of something or someone. It is a

118

♄ Saturn: Spiritual Master, Spiritual Friend

function of the natural human receptivity we are born with, which allows us to learn what we do not know. We cannot stifle our receptivity, or we could fall into a state of perception where we cannot receive realizations which will show us the way to a greater life.

Saturn, ruling fear, shows us how to expunge it. Saturn as the Ring-Pass-Not is where and how we meet all that separates us from our Divinity, dominion, and perfection. It is the boundary of our Soul awareness and expression which expands with the evolution of our loving heart. As we embrace Saturn's virtues, we see that all we fear is transitory and the uselessness of fearing anything. Fear will never do away with anything we fear, whereas eliminating fear demonstrates just how unreal and ineffective it is.

We cannot yield to this dangerous disease, or give it any more reality or power than it is due, which is none. Fear is a natural response, but also a learned one. When we confront our fear, we enter into a dark realm we've tried to avoid since infancy. There are very few things we are naturally afraid of, but there are many things we've learned to fear, like being alone, being with someone, not being with someone, being unloved, losing someone or something we value, not making enough money to live and thrive, being fired, evicted, or cut loose without resources. In all of these cases, we can eliminate fear by remembering it has no power over us. As we completely reject and repudiate it, we will experience that we are overcoming the power of fear to cripple our view. As we respond to what we fear with a positive focus, we move out of the realm of paralysis and anxiety, and quickly transcend our apprehensions.

I have found attitude is everything in overcoming this nonproductive and dangerous disease, since it is something we have control over. In my life, from the time I was a child (and feared many things, both real and imaginary) I have consistently found *courage* is the primary mental quality that supports us while facing those things that arouse apprehension and anxiety.

♄ Saturn: Spiritual Master, Spiritual Friend

This relates to the Sun as the natural antidote to a negative Saturn. The Sun is courage, light, and radiance. Having courage makes us feel stronger and more capable of handling whatever we confront. As we face our fears, they cease to trouble us, since by seeing how they have no power over our true Self, we dispel the illusion they are real at all. The Sun brings all things to light within its realm, up to and including the outer most limits where the visible gives way to the invisible. It shines even beyond the limits of what we can see. Our inner radiance is the means to dispel all darkness in our personal "solar system."

On the path to becoming Masters of the Wisdom in various areas of service, we will of necessity feel all the feelings there are to feel. This allows us to exercise self-discipline in the presence of unhelpful emotions, and not give away our power to negative feelings when they arise. As we become immune to fear, we then remain unaffected when we encounter it in others; we are no longer paralyzed by the disease, and can be a light of loving wisdom regardless of external conditions.

Fear is one of the four basic emotions which must be mastered if we are not to fall victim to its corrosive effects. We are told by a venerable source the other basic emotions are raw animal desire, vanity, and sensuousness, or the attachment to strong and temporarily gratifying sensations. These reside in the astral-emotional body, and one or more are present in all of the other emotions of the lower nature.

Fear is at the root of almost all anger, hatred, doubt, discouragement, and every other negative state of being. As we eradicate it, we cease being receptive to emotionally induced mental states leading us into error. We no longer magnetize events which bring forth dread, and even when we confront difficulty, we don't lose our mental equipoise which allows us a dispassionate way of viewing what we are faced with.

Until we train the mind and emotions to submit to the higher awareness that we eternally are, our desire mind will run us all over the map through its constantly

♄ Saturn: Spiritual Master, Spiritual Friend

changing focus on what it believes it wants. We take control over the desire mind by recognizing its patterns, and consciously choosing to still our lower desires and turn to higher things. As we acquire knowledge and awareness of greater aspirations, it becomes easier to put the Higher Self in the Captain's chair, and put the lower self into its suitable position as servant to our Higher Self.

Then we no longer have problems related to uncontrolled emotions at the mercy of our ignorance or lack of discipline. As we evolve, we learn the power we have to demonstrate a healthy and mature self-control, and eventually come out of any sense of being at the mercy of strong desires and feelings that have no productive purpose.

Self-control is not the same as repression. In facing our inner tendencies which undermine self-confidence, self-reliance, and the ability to grip life on our terms and live it to the fullest, we must learn to accept the power of the Higher Self to use our personality to exercise Divine Will, Love, and Intelligence to direct the lower mind and feelings into productive rather than non-productive tendencies.

Don't fall into distress at "not knowing." If there's a sense of drifting, reorient toward a clearer vision of what you're here to do in the larger scheme of things. Learn to feel which way your Divine receptivity is being pulled, and swim in that direction. You have nothing to lose but your fear and uncertainty.

As we destroy our ignorance, we banish fear. As we see our power to alter the course of events by how we respond to them, we destroy many superstitions and illusions. As we take back the power from the illusions, we eliminate their power to make us afraid.

Then we see that all fear, all malfunctioning of our mind, feelings, and actions, are the result of the undisciplined lower nature and a lack of self-control. That allows us to replace the habits of the lower ego with more productive responses, and over time, kill out the power of the lower ego to lead us into error. As we see the power of

♄ Saturn: Spiritual Master, Spiritual Friend

the lower nature diminish so it no longer dominates our lives, the lower ego becomes the servant of the Soul/Spirit that we are.

We occasionally have to confront the fear of what we believe others think about us. Desire for others' approval and avoiding others' disapproval is programmed into us from our earliest months on Earth. These exert a powerful influence on our subconscious mind, and affect our quality of life until we turn the loving light of clear understanding on those images of disapproval we dread and approval we desire.

This push and pull related to what others think is part of learning how to chart our own course, regardless of the world's approval or disapproval of how we act, think, or feel. While it's always pleasant to be with harmonious people who agree with us, it's also important to be able to stand firm in the universal truths we know when others don't like what we're saying, or don't approve of the path we've set for ourselves.

So learn to drop your fear, since it's a useless response. Learn to love yourself, and have the courage to express your lovingly wise Self to your world. You have nothing to lose but your fear. Expunge the root of fear and you will prevent a thousand problems from ever arising. Expunge the root of fear and you will find a power and clarity that will never desert you. There's no other time but NOW to expunge the patterns which allow fear to arise in your life.

WE ARE ALL ONE LIFE TOGETHER

Because we are all a part of humanity, we will feel what others feel. It's why when fear is in the air, we will all feel it, because we are One Life. The more aware we become, the more we will feel all the feelings we can tune into, both harmonious and difficult. What we're feeling may not necessarily be identified with a thing, which is why it's

♄ Saturn: Spiritual Master, Spiritual Friend

human to fall into confusion when we feel something unrelated to an obvious cause.

In mastering the emotional body, we are required to cultivate the ability to identify which feelings are ours in a deep personal sense, which are the feelings we're picking up when in the presence of others, and which feelings we're sensing because they are part of the holographic energy field. All sentient beings feel what they feel, and radiate their feelings into the general environment. Others who pick up on that feeling also experience it, whether or not they know the impetus for that feeling.

In learning to express our Loving Wise Intelligence, we must be clear about the sources of what we're feeling. Because the path to greater awareness leads through an expanded feeling sensitivity, we will tune into others' feelings, whether we want to or not or know why they are feeling that way. It is not enough simply to master our astral-emotional responses to internal issues; we must also learn how to demonstrate appropriate self-control and positive responses when we are in the presence of others who are having a hard time emotionally. As we feel all there is to feel while remaining unaffected by the negative feelings we encounter in the collective emotional fields we share with others, we learn how to move through life unafraid of any emotion, and can become a beacon of clarity, sanity, and courage in the midst of extreme conditions.

We are here to interact with others and as we learn, pay it forward. We cannot force our realizations on others, but must learn to share, just as others have shared with us. Along the way we learn to stay focused on the highest motive, the highest intention, and the most constructive and authentic way to be. Regardless of the external conditions we encounter, we are greater than those elements of material existence, and have the Divine Power to reorient away from fear and focus on those things which promise a more dynamic Love, Light, and Life.

Humanity is grappling with being at the cusp of the Great Age, where the past gives way to the future, and

♄ Saturn: Spiritual Master, Spiritual Friend

where the dilemmas of "belief versus doubt" are giving way to a unified field of vision for those who are cultivating a future-oriented way of perceiving reality. Relax into the uncertainty of life while simultaneously embracing the peace of knowing you have the ability to choose a way beyond fear. In the coming era, we will all know our special part to play in the completeness of the whole.

MOVING INTO OUR HIGHER DESTINY

The authorship of our existence begins with us. We are learning how to apply certain energies involving Divine Laws to fulfill Dharma in our world. We learn this many ways until we master those energies. The Higher Self, being the vehicle of our Soul/Spirit, doesn't take satisfaction in what it has accomplished, but seeks only to learn how to release creative energies in the future. It does not care about recognition, since it is already secure in its own Self-manifestation. As we live our Higher Self, we find we are one with others in a vast field of Loving Limitless Light within which we all live and breathe and have our Being.

As we mature spiritually, we are no longer bound, oppressed, confused, or powerless when confronting Dharma, and instead learn how to co-create our lives in a dance with Dharma. As we embrace a conscious co-creation of a life dedicated to fulfilling Dharma, we learn our power to reshape our Ring-Pass-Not. The Ring-Pass-Not expands with each lesson where we learn to apply wisdom, intelligence, and skill. Even though it is human to feel hassled by those things we are forced to deal with which push us to the limit, they are directly related to skills we're developing so we can express our Higher Self consistently and effectively in the future.

Impatience and any desire to skip over certain lessons are clear indicators of times when we are learning to be patient and thorough in antidoting these ego traps.

124

♄ Saturn: Spiritual Master, Spiritual Friend

As we learn about our power to expand the boundaries of our Ring-Pass-Not, we become more comfortable with who we are and what we're doing in any given moment. What we are willing to accept as we grow into ever greater awareness demonstrates our power to shape and expand the Ring-Pass-Not. As we move through experience and our understanding becomes deeper, broader, and more well-rounded, many perspectives shift. These shifts in perception adjust our Ring-Pass-Not, and we find we're only as limited as we need to be to master our understanding in those chapters of our eternal growth.

The Ring-Pass-Not is absolute, but infinitely expands with each step we master. It defines what is and is not "permitted," from the angle of our Soul's growth, both in terms of skills as well as comprehension. Throughout our life, we learn about different "Rings-Pass-Not," both personally and collectively, depending on our level of "response-ability." It's useful to keep in mind there are many Rings-Pass-Not, both in this existence and across our larger eternal path to Cosmic Consciousness.

The Ring-Pass-Not constrains the lower ego as it learns appropriate responses to karmas that fulfill Dharma. As we navigate within its boundaries, we are offered opportunities to confront and transcend our blind spots and limited ego-mind with its perceptions and assumptions that hinder or needlessly limit us. Countless teachings of Sages and true Spiritual Teachers make it clear there are many limitations of ego and matter to master. Doing this effectively requires imagination, accepting that we have limits we need to examine, and a willingness to strive to grow beyond our inabilities. Much that seems fearful or burdensome when we are trying to imagine what we believe we must do becomes easier once we begin learning and practicing those skills in circumstances appropriate to our level of development.

By claiming the ability to grow into a spiritually responsible awareness and function in the world, and finding the right disciplines and skills appropriate to fulfilling Dharma, we become the manifestation of Spirit in the

♄ Saturn: Spiritual Master, Spiritual Friend

world. Saturn guides us as we learn these things, allowing us to leave behind limiting cultural biases and claim the transpersonal freedom that eliminates them from our consciousness. Then our path to freedom becomes crystal clear.

DHARMA AND THE RING PASS NOT

Because life on Earth is impermanent, it's pretty much one long series of goodbyes, whether to people, activities, dreams, memories, or all the other things we experience while we're alive on Earth. However, since Nature abhors a vacuum, inevitably we'll attract, and be attracted to, new forms of these throughout our lives. This helps us learn a full glass cannot accept more water, but an empty one can, and an open hand can be filled, but a hand clenching something tightly cannot receive anything.

The Ring-Pass-Not forces us to deal with our apprehension of the unknown, of leaving behind old comfortable "skins of personality" (Saturn rules the skin and bones in Medical Astrology), abandoning old rules and crystalized life structures that have become sclerotic, inhibiting our growth as Eternal Soul/Spirits in the material world. It constrains us until we break free of mental and emotional echo chambers and identify with our Higher Self. As we practice referencing the Higher Self and make the lower self its vehicle of expression, we are unbound from lesser things.

We live within our Ring-Pass-Not which expands each time we evolve and demonstrate the ability to express our evolving Self to the world in ever more skilled ways. So the Ring-Pass-Not of our childhood became the Ring-Pass-Not of our adulthood, somehow the same and somehow changed. As we grew, it grew, and as we learned to embrace a greater truth, goodness, and beauty, we saw these take shape to the furthest reaches of our ability to bring them into manifestation.

126

♄ Saturn: Spiritual Master, Spiritual Friend

To get a vaster perspective of life patterns and how they shaped the circumstances of our growth, it's useful to take a look at how we were limited when younger. As we examine what bound us to attitudes, assumptions, fears, and frustrations when we were children, we can remember events which spurred us to grow beyond them. With deep reflection over time, we can catch glimpses about how our Higher Self has been leading our lower self out of fear through many twists and turns on our "Hero's Journey."

Think about everything that ever made you afraid, or feel oppressed. Those were moments when you experienced your Ring-Pass-Not. Think about every "hard truth" or "bottom line" lesson you went through. Think about every time you had to take responsibility for charting your own course, or doing those things you knew you had to do, regardless of others' thoughts, beliefs, and opinions. Those were the moments when your Ring-Pass-Not expanded because you accepted your power to take charge of your life, your karma, and your Dharma.

See how every time you took command of your power your life changed. Your capabilities grew, your ability to respond expanded in ways you never anticipated, and you became aware of new rules, disciplines, and structures which were perfect for your evolved Self. As we learn to shed old skins of personality which limit us, over time we become more comfortable with moving through temporary binding circumstances as we express various facets of our Higher Self. It's all part of learning how to be "perfectly human," knowing what we can take responsibility for, and what we cannot. Sometimes it gets strange or difficult, but we always have the ability to respond thoughtfully, intelligently, and consciously generate positivity and wisdom.

℞ Saturn: Spiritual Master, Spiritual Friend

REFLECTIONS ON THE RING-PASS-NOT

Since the Ring-Pass-Not is such an important part of our process of evolving from ignorance to greater awareness, and from limitation to our sense of eternal freedom, I thought a few self-reflective questions would be appropriate.

1. When was the first time in your childhood or young adulthood when you broke free of a limitation, or were able to go beyond a boundary (physical, emotional, mental, and/or spiritual) opening a new perspective or world of activity?
2. Which events brought forth your greatest sense of liberation or freedom? How did you grow in power or clarity before, during, and after you got beyond the old role or limitation?
3. Remember the times when you realized with extraordinary clarity that you really, *really* should not "go there" or "do that." What did it teach you about listening to the inner voice, and how did it help you in other situations you didn't need to be involved in?
4. When you were frustrated and unable to reach some goals or roles you wanted to play, what did you realize about your limitations, and how they created your beliefs, or how your beliefs influenced your limitations?
5. If your goals were unrealistic, why were they unrealistic? If you had a realistic role or goal you aspired to, did you learn the things you needed to learn to become the role or achieve the goal? What did you do to get beyond the limitation?
6. Which limitations in your life are more boon than bondage?
7. Take an inventory of your assumptions about your duties, binding obligations, skills, and belief systems. While these have served your purpose in some way up to now, are they still serving your higher

♄ Saturn: Spiritual Master, Spiritual Friend

aspirations in some way? If not, what can you learn that will help you transition from those that don't serve your ideals to those that will?

8. Which of your limitations came from self-doubt, and which came from self-awareness?

9. Given when we pass through some doors we can never go back, if you want to "break on through to the other side," whatever that might mean to you, are you will in live on the other side" for the rest of your life?

10. What is your image of your greatest spiritual ideal of effectiveness? How has your life prepared you to live your ideal? What can you do to train to express your ideal in a concrete way?

♄ Saturn: Spiritual Master, Spiritual Friend

♄ Saturn: Spiritual Master, Spiritual Friend

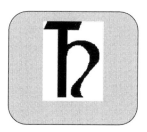

PART II

♄ Saturn: Spiritual Master, Spiritual Friend

♄ Saturn: Spiritual Master, Spiritual Friend

SATURN TRANSITS
AN INTRODUCTION

In Part Two of this work, we'll examine various types of Saturn transits, and the possible events and challenges we experience during those important life changing periods. Often, when we're dealing with difficulty during a Saturn transit, it can feel like we have been "trying the wrong way" before now, and find new approaches so we don't feel trapped by circumstances. Often there is also the sense that things are not happening "fast enough," along with the feeling like we've learned a lot along the way but don't quite know how to use our knowledge and experience to deal with what's happening.

During a Saturn transit of any sort, it's useful to remember we can't push the river, and must relax into the long-wave process. These are times when we can complete many things if we simply persist, but it requires us to find the right rhythm of activity, doing each part of the work in the right way and time. Then we wind up exactly where we need to be.

All of Saturn's lessons are related to the core theme that each of us is accountable to and responsible for ourselves, and how we choose to express qualities of energy, thoughts, words and actions. In other words, each one of us casts pebbles in the pond of Life, and at various points confront the ripples coming back to center. A Saturn transit brings us opportunities to see how past causes have created specific effects, and offers us opportunities to leave behind lesser things and embrace our higher Destiny, even if we don't know what that is. Saturn always brings us opportunities to embrace a more mature view of how we understand truth, and offers insights into the wisdom of each stage of our evolving process.

♄ Saturn: Spiritual Master, Spiritual Friend

Often as we learn to master basic lessons we want to know everything as quickly as possible. Then we begin to explore information and experience in a random way, and frequently lose our bearings, leading us to confrontations with unresolved psychological issues, where we respond ineffectively and create some real problems for ourselves and others. Through those circumstances we realize submitting to Saturn's guidance is a real blessing, since we CANNOT overleap what we must learn from Saturn which keeps bringing us back to basics.

With each turn of the wheel, Saturn helps us reference our bottom line so we can see how each lesson presenting itself during a Saturn transit occurs within the context of larger lessons related to what we are here to learn about what is over and done, and what is yet to come. Saturn transits are times when we can resolve whatever has become burdensome and move forward freed of the deadwood of obsolete rules, limits, obligations, and assumptions. Then life becomes lighter indeed!

As you understand "the whole cycle," and how Saturn transits mark important times of shifting emphasis within those cycles, you will get a larger view of how your life has unfolded the way it has, and why you confronted certain crucial decisions at key points in your evolution. You will also see how the inner changes marked by your progressed Lunar cycle relate to the outer world events indicated by Saturn transits, and come to a broader understanding of the dance between your inner Self and the world you live in.

CHAPTER 6

THE SATURN CYCLE CONJUNCTIONS

Over the years I've observed countless people become very anxious and worried when transiting Saturn makes a conjunction, square, or opposition to their Ascendant or planets in their charts. While Saturn transits can bring tough lessons, it never brings us anything we don't need, and is the timekeeper for major beginnings and endings, as well as the significant shifts within any major life cycle.

As we know, the planets merely represent our inner functions operating through various external actions and experiences, each associated with a planet's department of labor. Saturn transits mark the timing of various critical challenges to parts of our personality so we can integrate all of them into a smooth running life, achieving those things we need to as we navigate the River of Life.

For better or worse, Saturn transits bring the results of how we have chosen to embody each planetary function. As it conjuncts each planet in our chart, it brings the pressure of completion. We see how we have actualized that energy over a long cycle, and must close some things so others can open. Saturn transits make the relative health of different parts of our personality very clear, guiding each to a better function if we consciously cooperate with the process.

♄ Saturn: Spiritual Master, Spiritual Friend

A Saturn transit is when we get clear about who we are, and who we aren't, and confront whether our Saturn function is leading us into oppression or power and freedom. As Saturn conjuncts each planet, we can leave behind restrictive, unreasonable, or immature expectations and belief systems associated with that planet, and process experience into wisdom leading us to saner, wiser forms of self-expression. We learn what we must accept so we can live more effectively in the future, and can take the long view about how time and experience now require a more mature and appropriate expression of each planetary energy.

Saturn leads us to get our act together so our life actually works fairly well, since the conjunctions, squares, and oppositions of and to Saturn make it clear what we have to do to fine tune our responses to circumstances and figure out what we need to learn. Even though we certainly learn favorable Saturn lessons during harmonious aspects to our natal Saturn, as well as from transiting Saturn to our planets, we learn advanced Saturn skills during the frictional aspects. When a Saturn transit brings up feelings of being jammed or frustrated, it's the perfect practicum for us to demonstrate how well we've mastered Saturn's strengths and virtues appropriate to those situations.

Through Saturn we understand time as the structural framework for how our life lessons unfold so that each challenge to growth serves the evolutionary need of that time. By observing the issues associated with various Saturn transits, we are given continual "real time" feedback about how we can adjust to be more effective. The common thread in all crucial Saturn lessons is to be realistic in understanding that something is fulfilled, and we stand on the threshold of a new way of experiencing a planetary energy. Since many of the most stressful collisions of the lower self with the Higher Self are associated with Saturn transits, let's begin by examining what we can expect when Saturn makes conjunctions to natal planets and the Ascendant.

137

♄ Saturn: Spiritual Master, Spiritual Friend

CONJUNCTIONS - A REFRESHER

As I introduced in Chapter Two, when Saturn (or any planet) comes close to another planet or significant point in the chart, we say Saturn is conjunct (at or near the same longitudinal degree as) that point. This leads us to a crucial concept in calculating aspects between planets, which are called "orbs." Orbs are the maximum number of degrees from an exact angle creating the aspect effect. Anything between the outer limit and the exact angle is the "orb."

Conjunctions and oppositions get maximum orb, usually anywhere from 10-15 degrees from exact, depending on the planets involved. The Sun and Moon get the widest orbs of aspect influence, and so we may find a planet conjunct our Sun or Moon while still being a fair distance from those heavenly bodies. It's why a conjunction effect happens even when it's a number of degrees away and still forming, or getting closer.

Forming conjunctions indicate impending energy we are beginning to confront on a more or less constant basis. A forming conjunction marks the end of the cycle launched at the previous conjunction. The exact conjunction finishes the form of the old, and introduces a new beginning. Since all conjunctions are associated with some type of fusion, exact conjunctions are the time we're in the heart of that "fusion" or rebirth energy. Separating conjunctions show we've gone through the fusion or rebirth, and have started the next cycle of unfoldment.

We definitely feel the influence of Saturn when it's in the same sign as one or more of our planets, regardless of how distant they are from each other. Saturn in a sign affects all planets in that sign, whether it's forming or separating from a conjunction to those planets.

Any time Saturn conjuncts any of our planets we are led through events and decisions transforming us for the rest of our lives. It is why the period after Saturn

♄ Saturn: Spiritual Master, Spiritual Friend

conjuncts our Sun, Ascendant, or any other planet is radically different than the time before those conjunctions occurred. When Saturn conjuncts our Ascendant or a planet, it marks the end of an old way of defining those energies, and the beginning of a new long term cycle of learning how to express those energies in more effective and thoughtful ways.

Saturn conjunctions are times to get ready, prepare, and accept the lessons of restructuring those life areas and our attitudes about them. Conjunctions always indicate we are ending one life phase and moving into some kind of new start, closing some doors and opening others. Our future happiness and fulfillment in these renewed, restructured life areas depends entirely on how we view the potential.

TRANSITING SATURN CONJUNCT OUR SUN

When transiting Saturn conjuncts our natal Sun, our Light is confirmed, and we understand our life within the structure we confront at that time. Our long term experience comes to our Light, so our Illumination takes a more mature form. In the case of a dysfunctional Saturn or Sun, rigidity, fear, and authoritarian tendencies may appear, either in us or in another we confront. If we find these coming up internally, we have to find a way to restructure our power in a newer, more fruitful form. If we find ourselves dealing with another who is rigid, fearful, or authoritarian, then all we can do is demonstrate spiritual maturity as we find completion and bless the passage.

Saturn conjunct the Sun is when we reap the results and rewards of living our integrity and Light over time, or feel oppressed as a result of past self-betrayals and accepting limitations which weren't ours to begin with. Saturn in the same sign as our Sun may bring us recognition for what we have accomplished and mark a

139

♄ Saturn: Spiritual Master, Spiritual Friend

time when we restructure how we view illumination and the light we give to others, as well as how we live our heart's higher purpose. Things end, but only those things our Light no longer needs to shine forth of its own authority with renewed clarity.

As with all Saturn cycles, it is the time when a major 29+ year life cycle is over and another begins. When Saturn conjuncts the Sun, we get exactly what we deserve for prior long term efforts, and find newer, more mature and rewarding ways of living life and expressing our Light. It indicates a time when we graduate into a different sense of the value of age and experience.

Whether a climax of achievement or recognition, or the end of a long effort bringing apparent failure, frustration, or a sense of unfulfilled potential, a Saturn conjunction lets us know it's harvest time. Whether a peak of fulfillment or the end of a way of life, it is a time to plan anew, revise methods, goals, and expectancies, and set a new course toward more realistic, achievable, and fulfilling goals.

I found when Saturn visited my Sun, it brought me some very concrete and dramatic results of how I had defined my Light/Life before then. Each gave me the keys to unlock doors leading to knowledge that I had accomplished something of worth, and it was time to move on. My experiences had led me to a deepened perspective about "wise choices" and I knew an old life was gone forever.

Saturn conjunct (or square or opposition) our Sun, tests our ability to shine our Light and live life on our terms. We are challenged to trust what we have developed in the way of enlightened maturity, and accept our power to act as we know we need to. When Saturn makes heavy aspects to our Sun and we confront difficulties and hard realizations, we cannot put blame on outer conditions or people. These are periods to confront worldly realities rather than withdraw from worldly contacts, taking life more seriously and personal biases less seriously. We can find important insights about how well we know ourselves, and

♄ Saturn: Spiritual Master, Spiritual Friend

how much we're willing to change the parts of our life which are frustrating our Light, heart, and ability to shine in the world.

TRANSITING SATURN CONJUNCT OUR MOON

When transiting Saturn conjuncts our natal Moon, our personal feelings deepen, we become much more introspective, and we restructure our habits and ways of experiencing day to day life. Many have to confront fear, insecurity, or discouragement under this transit. By noting any negative emotional responses accompanying this transit, we are offered chances to reprioritize how we are or not taking care of ourselves and others appropriately.

Saturn conjunct our Moon shows us who we really are behind the defenses we have created to feel secure in our "shell of personality." It can bring very deep (and often heavy) insights and feelings, since the inner self is confronting hard realities. This can lead to a profound sense of the gap between how we would like to respond and our inability to generate that response.

During this time we must confront the world as it is, and not as we hope, wish, assume, or imagine it to be. We are challenged to find new ways to express what we truly care about on our terms. In short, Saturn conjunct the Moon forces us to reevaluate our life "care plan," and find a cure to any emotional heaviness accompanying this transit. It is a serious time, and we take life very seriously when Saturn visits our Moon.

This transit brings us profound truths about who we are, and through the self-knowledge we are offered opportunities to grow into a more secure existence. The emotional maturity resulting from our experiences will yield an emotional strength, clarity and connectedness with ourselves which will never desert us.

When Saturn conjuncts the Moon, we have to de-emphasize our rules, "shoulds," or duties so we can take

𝟤 Saturn: Spiritual Master, Spiritual Friend

care of ourselves more effectively, as well as let go of sentimentalities and unproductive habits which have become too calcified to endure any longer, or no longer matter to us. While it can be a hard time, this lasts only as long as it takes to restructure the emotional body so we can take care of ourselves and not feel deprived. These periods help us find new things we care about and new connectedness with life and our needs.

Saturn visiting our Moon always begins a new phase in our personal lives and relationships, where we say good-bye to a very intimate and primal part of the past and welcome a more mature "package of personality." As we leave behind old feelings, habits, and personality traits, we can embrace new ones which nurture who we have become.

Saturn's heavy aspects to our Moon offer us chances to take a hard look at our emotional assumptions, and see how they're related to childhood and early adult personality patterns. It is an excellent time to re-evaluate unconscious or subconscious needs related to the family and cultural matrix, and leave behind emotional patterns which no longer serve us. Though sometimes these periods can feel limiting, restrictive, and bring some hard truths, they also accompany emotional and experiential rewards as well as a security in those who have cultivated an inner connectedness with their Higher Self. In Chapter Seven we'll go into greater detail about the conjunctions, squares, and oppositions of the Saturn cycle, and what we can expect when it makes those angles to our planets.

TRANSITING SATURN CONJUNCT
OUR MERCURY, VENUS, MARS, AND JUPITER

When transiting Saturn conjoins our natal Mercury, our thinking becomes more structured and profound, or rigid and dogmatic. How we coordinate our affairs is organized into a workable routine. New routines are

♄ Saturn: Spiritual Master, Spiritual Friend

introduced replacing old ones, or we struggle with an order that seems unyielding and has become too confining. We learn what we really know and don't know, and whether our thinking is too narrow, rule-bound, or pessimistic. We become more thoughtful, and how we understand, interpret, and communicate information becomes more important.

It's a great time for studying, reading, writing, or any other mental discipline. If we are open, transiting Saturn conjunct natal Mercury deepens our understanding, and indicates a time when our minds are more naturally focused on serious matters, and more important subjects. These are excellent times to learn techniques of concentration and organized critical thinking skills. All forms of mental and verbal training are favored, and we can make parts of our life work more efficiently than they did in the past.

When Saturn conjuncts natal Mercury, it's a particularly good time to change how we say what we say so that our words have deeper meaning and affirm what is in our and others' best interests. It's a time when objectivity yields great rewards, and any effort dedicated to seeing life in more mature ways brings gravitas to future forms of self-expression. Saturn's influence on Mercury offers us long term training where we may be "led to our Soul," and weave or re-weave how we move between matter, Soul, and Spirit.

When transiting Saturn conjuncts our natal Venus, our values change and evolve, as well as those things we like and why we like them. They are periods when we find different, more efficient ways to use what we have, and often find ourselves wanting to eliminate the vanities and superficialities of life. These are times to let go of extravagance, and detach from unsatisfying people and things.

During the time Saturn touches our Venus, our relationships change dramatically, and we drop obsolete people who are more trouble than they're worth or no longer reflect who we really are. Any major conjunction (or

♄ Saturn: Spiritual Master, Spiritual Friend

square or opposition) by Saturn to our Venus cleans out relationships and things that no longer express our evolved way of living our Venus function, and when those periods are over, everyone and everything in our lives are more meaningful, valuable, pleasing, or worthwhile.

Saturn conjunct Moon or Venus may accompany hard lessons in human relations, but it frees us to take care of our likes and needs appropriately. These are times to take a slow, steady, and realistic approach to people and a hard look at those who make us unhappy or trigger negative emotional responses. They provide clear information about who to leave, or what we have to confront to make our lives and relationships more happy, authentic, or fulfilling. Over time, any losses will yield more rewarding relationships appropriate to our evolved state of relational maturity.

When transiting Saturn conjuncts our natal Mars, our energies are somewhat restricted. We have to examine how and why we are aggravated or hassled, and take steps to create structured ways to deal with the release of the pressure before it explodes or implodes. We cannot ignore or stuff down frustration, impatience, or agitation, nor can we simply let these run loose.

It's always a time to reorganize how we respond to what we think we're supposed to be doing and slow down! It's a great time to see how effective you are, and how you can adjust your energy to make it work smoothly and efficiently in attaining your objectives. Saturn conjunct natal Mars challenges us to be more deliberate in how we do those things we must, and evaluate the potential long term results of our initiatives and efforts. These periods show us how to make time, patience, and organization our allies in implementing our plans.

It is an excellent period to take a long mature look at any toxic anger we're holding internally, and do what we must to bring up and expunge both the anger and the sources of anger which are corrosive to our Higher Self. Saturn conjunct our natal Mars certainly demonstrates how disciplined we are or aren't. Force nothing, and be patient,

♄ Saturn: Spiritual Master, Spiritual Friend

steady, and precise in applying your energies with maximum efficiency. Remember persistence and determination often succeed when other methods don't. Knowing when to rest and stop pushing are paramount during Saturn's contacts with Mars.

Transiting Saturn conjunct natal Jupiter restructures our imagination, the promise of a greater future, our philosophy and spiritual beliefs, our sense of life as an ever expanding adventure of limitless opportunities, and all the other areas ruled by Jupiter. Some things are cut back, while other things are pursued in a structured way. Experience is incorporated into the broader view of opportunity, and pragmatic plans can be made that will pay off over time.

Saturn's power of persistence with an eye to long term rewards is the means by which Jupiter's promise is made real. Saturn visiting Jupiter is not a time to expect quick gains, but rather a period when organized plans and reliable methods are the means to achieve success. There is a need to take it slow and steady as we work with what could be possible and methodically bring it into actuality.

Transiting Saturn on our Jupiter is a time when our larger view of truth, philosophy, or morality becomes more organized or dogmatic, depending on our mindset and imagination and how willing we are to take a larger view of a more universal understanding. We can see how time and discipline have brought forth a broader potential as a function of life experiences, and using the understanding we've achieved, move into greater life adventures through focusing our imagination so we are clear about what we can realistically accomplish related to our higher purposes.

These are times when our philosophy matures, as well as our sense of what we believe to be true. They can also bring us a long range spiritual discipline, or a teacher who profoundly impacts our spiritual view and life.

****

♄ Saturn: Spiritual Master, Spiritual Friend

A Saturn conjunction to our planets has the effect of showing us which parts of personality we need to shore up and restructure to be effective in the future. As Grant Lewi put it, it is when "the chickens come home to roost," for good or ill, based in the quality of our effort since the last time it conjuncted that planet or our Ascendant. When we confront difficulty during a Saturn transit, we are being made aware that something in our life structure has outlived its time. As we fulfill various potentials, some parts of our lives become old or stale, and we are shown it's time to get closure. Saturn transits help us see when an old potential has been fulfilled for better and/or for worse, and it's time to move forward into a more satisfying future.

So yes, things seem weightier during any Saturn transit. That is not surprising, since Saturn symbolizes density. Through the heaviness we feel while going through a Saturn lesson, we are slowly but surely taught to see what is obsolete and no longer needed. This allows us to eliminate, methodically and deliberately, unfulfilling ways of living life. All difficult periods challenge us to find new ways to live our evolved spiritual integrity.

SATURN CONJUNCT THE ASCENDANT

Up to now we've discussed possible ways transiting Saturn conjunct a planet in our chart could manifest. In this section, we'll explore what we experience when it gets near our Ascendant, as well as how and when Saturn brought its lessons to different Ascendant signs.

This is one of an extremely important Saturn cycle, since the Ascendant is associated with our self-image, self-awareness, and "window on the world." The Ascendant is our orientation to the specialized departments of life represented by the houses. When Saturn visits our Ascendant, we take a more serious look at who we think we are, what we believe we know about ourselves, who we have become, and those things we are yet to do.

146

♄ Saturn: Spiritual Master, Spiritual Friend

Saturn conjunct the Ascendant is a time when we grow up, become more serious than we used to be, or at least more "matter of fact." We accept obligations more readily, which is why we have to get clear about what is and is not ours to do. Our self-image matures as a function of long term experience.

Saturn visiting the Ascendant often accompanies a new learning rigor, and a sense that "we're not a kid anymore." Often we may feel or seem to be older than we were before then. We definitely feel our age under a Saturn transit, as well as a sense of the seriousness of life, and eliminate everything we're struggling with which is more trouble than it's worth. It's a time when we realize we are not as we used to be.

The choices we make when Saturn visits our Ascendant bring new ways of being in relationships, including our relationship with the ego-self and the Higher Self, as well as the world. When Saturn visits the Ascendant, we know something is complete, and are ready to use the wisdom-experience we've accumulated in the past in new ways.

The Ascendant represents our specialized unique purpose of Being. It distinguishes us from everyone else born on our birthday, and shows the qualities we share with all others who have a similar Ascendant. It is our self-referencing self-awareness, our window on inner and outer reality. Since nothing clarifies things better than Saturn, when Saturn is near or on the Ascendant, we awaken to a whole new self-awareness and the realization that a part of our old self-image has left forever. When we know we are not as we were, then we can rise to the occasion of becoming a more effective expression of our unique role to play in the world.

Saturn conjunct the Ascendant often accompanies some very important changes in life. It can bring a significant birth or death, a meeting or loss of someone who played or will play a major part in our lives, or accepting a more important role to play in the world. It leads some to a deeper, more sober sense of purpose, as

147

℞ Saturn: Spiritual Master, Spiritual Friend

well as opportunities to accept some role with greater or heavier responsibilities they might not have accepted before then.

These are periods when we confront the need to accept new long range tasks, or forms of training or retraining allowing us to express our expertise in new ways. It may mark the end of a job or even a career and the beginning of a new one. It's definitely a time when elders or those in power play a more important role in the life, or a time when we are recognized as an authority in some way because of experience, knowledge, or understanding.

Throughout our lives, Saturn *will* conjunct our Ascendant (and all the planets) at least once, and often twice or even three times if we live to an old age or experience a conjunction when we're very young. Obviously, when we are young and not the authors of our lives, Saturn transits play out through the adults in our family and cultural constellations. In every case, each time it conjuncts our Ascendant, we end an old way of seeing ourselves and awaken to a new role to play in our world.

So who has been under this influence, and when? The rest of this chapter takes a look at the different groups who have been learning the important lessons of maturing as Saturn has conjuncted or will conjunct their Ascendants. Depending on your exact Ascendant degree, you will have to adjust the following dates somewhat, while keeping in mind you started your changes at least a year before it went over your Ascendant, and once it actually conjuncted your Ascendant it moved into your first house, thus extending the effect for at least one to two years afterward.

That's why those with the last half of a sign rising will still feel the effects of Saturn in their first house when Saturn moves into the first half of the next sign. Saturn will still be in their first house, but it will be in a different sign. This gives a dual tone to their first house Self-reinvention experience.

For example, if someone has 20 Libra on the Ascendant, they will begin to experience Saturn on their

148

♄ Saturn: Spiritual Master, Spiritual Friend

Ascendant when it first enters Libra. It will become focused when Saturn is in the middle and later degrees of Libra, but the experience of Saturn in the first house will continue during the time Saturn is in the first 20 degrees of Scorpio, since using an equal house division of the chart, Saturn will still be in their first house.

Continuing the example, if someone has 26 Scorpio on the Ascendant, they will experience Saturn conjunct their Ascendant as early as when Saturn first enters Scorpio, and will continue to feel Saturn conjunct the Ascendant through its entire transit of that sign. However, the influence will extend through the time Saturn is in the first 26 degrees of Sagittarius, since Saturn would still be in their first house, even though in a different sign than the Ascendant.

So let's take a look at when Saturn transited through the signs, and when it touched the lives of those with Ascendants in a given sign. Look at these times as the beginning of a new learning rigor, or new maturity, self-discipline, self-image, or role in the world.

♄ Saturn: Spiritual Master, Spiritual Friend

SATURN TRANSITS THROUGH THE SIGNS
1967-2055

Saturn Conjunct Ascendant Dates	
April 1996 - March 1997	Early Aries
March 1997 - March 1998	Mid Aries
March 1998 - June 1998	Late Aries
June 1998 - October 1998	Early Taurus
October 1998 - February 1999	Late Aries
Before that, Saturn was in Aries from March 1967 through April 1969; it will again visit Aries from late May through August 2025, and February 2026 through April 2028.	
March 1999 - May 1999	Early Taurus
May 1999 - May 2000	Mid Taurus
May 2000 - August 2000	Late Taurus
August 2000 - October 2000	Early Gemini
October 2000 - April 2001	Late Taurus
Before that, Saturn was in Taurus from May 1969 through June 1971 and January-February 1972; it will again visit Taurus from April 2028 through May 2030.	

150

♄ Saturn: Spiritual Master, Spiritual Friend

April 2001 - July 2001	Early Gemini
July 2001 - December 2001	Mid Gemini
December 2001 - March 2002	Early Gemini
March 2002 - June 2003	Late Gemini

Before that, Saturn was in Gemini from June 1971 through early January 1972, late February 1972 through July 1973, and from January through April 1974; it will again visit Gemini from June 2030 and July 2032.

June 2003 - August 2003	Early Cancer
September 2003 - December 2003	Mid Cancer
January 2004 - April 2004	Early Cancer
April 2004 - July 2004	Mid Cancer
August 2004 - July 2005	Late Cancer

Before that, Saturn was in Cancer from August through early January 1974, April 1974 through September 1975, and January through early June 1976; it will again visit Cancer from July 2032 through August 2034, and February through May 2035.

July 2005 - October 2005	Early Leo
October 2005 - December 2005	Mid Leo
January 2006 - June 2006	Early Leo

151

♄ Saturn: Spiritual Master, Spiritual Friend

July 2006 - September 2006	Mid Leo
September 2006 - February 2007	Late Leo
March 2007 - May 2007	Mid Leo
June 2007 - September 2007	Late Leo

Before that, Saturn was in Leo from September 1975 through January 1976, June 1976 through November 1977, and January through July 1978; it will again visit Leo from late August 2034 through February 2035, May 2035 through October 2036, and February through early July 2037.

September 2007 - August 2008	Early Virgo
August 2008 - November 2008	Mid Virgo
November 2008 - February 2009	Late Virgo
February 2009 - August 2009	Mid Virgo
August 2009 - October 2009	Late Virgo
October 2009 - April 2010	Early Libra
April 2010 - July 2010	Late Virgo

Before that, Saturn was in Virgo from November 1977 through January 1978, and late July 1978 through September 1980; it will again visit Virgo from October 2036 through February 2037, and July 2037 through early September 2039.

| July 2010 - October 2010 | Early Libra |

152

℞ Saturn: Spiritual Master, Spiritual Friend

October 2010 - October 2011	Mid Libra
October 2011 - October 2012	Late Libra

Before that, Saturn was in Libra from mid-September 1980 through November 1982, and May through August 1982; it will again visit Libra from September 2039 through November 2041, and late June 2042 through July 2042.

October 2012 - January 2013	Early Scorpio
January 2013 - April 2013	Mid Scorpio
April 2013 - September 2013	Early Scorpio
October 2013 - December 2013	Mid Scorpio
December 2013 - May 2014	Late Scorpio
May 2014 - September 2014	Mid Scorpio
September 2014 - December 2014	Late Scorpio
December 2014 - June 2015	Early Sagittarius
June 2015 - September 2015	Late Scorpio

Before that, Saturn was in Scorpio from late November 1982 through early May 1983, and late August 1983 through November 1985; it will again visit Scorpio from November 2041 through June 2042, July 2042 through February 2044, and late March through October 2044.

September 2015 - December 2015	Early Sagittarius

153

♄ Saturn: Spiritual Master, Spiritual Friend

December 2015 - July 2016	Mid Sagittarius
July 2016 - August 2016	Early Sagittarius
September 2016 - December 2016	Mid Sagittarius
December 2016 - December 2017	Late Sagittarius

Before that, Saturn was in Sagittarius from mid-November 1985 through mid-February 1988, and mid-June through mid-November 1988; it will again visit Sagittarius from late February 2044 through late March 2044, November 2044 through late January 2047, and July through October 2047..

December 2017 - December 2018	Early Capricorn
December 2018 - April 2019	Mid Capricorn
April 2019 - May 2019	Late Capricorn
May 2019 - December 2019	Mid Capricorn
December 2019 - March 2020	Late Capricorn
March 2020 - June 2020	Early Aquarius
July 2020 - December 2020	Late Capricorn

Before that, Saturn was in Capricorn from mid-February 1988 through mid-June 1988, and November 1988 through early February 1991; it will again visit Capricorn from late January 2047 through early July 2047, and late October 2047 through January 2050.

℞ Saturn: Spiritual Master, Spiritual Friend

December 2020 - March 2021	Early Aquarius
March 2021 - August 2021	Mid Aquarius
August 2021 - December 2021	Early Aquarius
December 2021 - March 2022	Mid Aquarius
March 2022 - September 2022	Late Aquarius
September 2022 - December 2022	Mid Aquarius
December 2022 - March 2023	Late Aquarius

Before that, Saturn was in Aquarius from mid-February 1991 through May 1993, and July 1993 through January 1994; it will again visit Aquarius from late January through April 2052, and August 2052 through January 2052.

March 2023 - February 2024	Early Pisces
March 2024 - February 2025	Mid Pisces
February 2025 - May 2025	Late Pisces
September 2025 - February 2026	Late Pisces

Before that, Saturn was in Pisces from late May through June 1993, and late January 1994 through early April 1996; it will again visit Pisces from April through August 2052, and January 2052 through March 2055.

155

℔ Saturn: Spiritual Master, Spiritual Friend

CHAPTER 7

THE SATURN CYCLE

SQUARES AND OPPOSITIONS

So far, we've explored what Saturn conjunctions bring and the signs and age groups most affected by Saturn's "destiny shaping" quality over the past 50 years. Now we'll explore how the squares and oppositions fit into a larger pattern set into motion at Saturn's conjunction with the Ascendant and our planets, since all Saturn conjunctions mark the end of a long cycle of self-expression and the beginning of a new one. All planetary cycles are set into motion by the various conjunctions, and each has its waxing square, its opposition, and its waning square in its "whole cycle."

THE WHOLE CYCLE

The first half of the any cycle builds whatever the cycle set into motion at the conjunction. It is a time when the purpose and "meaning" of the cycle builds form and "embraces the potential." At the opposition, what has been built comes to the surface in its field of expression. It marks a major phase shift in the whole cycle, where we confront the need to make important adjustments on the basis of emergent circumstances.

The second half of any cycle brings forms to fulfillment, and "captures the actual." As the cycle nears its

♄ Saturn: Spiritual Master, Spiritual Friend

end, it creates and releases the seeds of future potential which will sprout anew at the next conjunction. From the conjunction to the opposition of any planet to any other planet or the Ascendant, all possible aspects (angular relationships) are made. These are called "waxing" aspects. From the opposition to the next conjunction, all the aspects are made again, but in reverse order. These are called "waning" aspects.

This "mirroring" of how the aspects of the first half of a cycle are repeated but in reverse order in the second half of the cycle demonstrates a larger pattern of "weaving and unweaving" the fabric in how any given thing is made manifest. All of the waxing and waning aspects made throughout an entire cycle represent a sequence of "pulses," demonstrating specific phases of development. Each of them involves different facets of the purpose of the cycle as it evolves and is revealed at various stages within the cycle.

I regard the conjunction, waxing square, opposition, and waning square as the primary "stations" in the whole cycle. Conjunctions are points where a cycle is birthed. From the conjunction, we move through various aspects of growth, specialization, and conscious choice leading to events through which we realize the fulfillment of the cycle.

The waxing (lower) square is a time when we move out of the first waxing quadrant and the hemisphere of "self" into the hemisphere of the "not self" and the world of interactions. At the waxing square the emerging cycle is still "below the surface" but encounters circumstances and changes in a new arena of life activities and experiences which are not solely self-determined and self-influenced.

From that point, we continue through various phases of choice and change, specialization, stabilization, and frictional adjustment in this second waxing quadrant until we reach the opposition. This marks the end of the first half of the cycle, and the beginning of the second. This is the point where we take a new look at the potential as it has developed, and adjust to focus the trajectory on the attainable ideal.

℞ Saturn: Spiritual Master, Spiritual Friend

At the opposition, there is another hemispheric phase shift, where the developing cycle moves from a subjective experience into a more objective or public self-expression. What was hidden is now seen and known within the realm of "not self." It marks a point where the process begins to fulfill itself in ways which can be seen by all those participating in or impacted by that cycle.

The opposition marks a point in the cycle where factors supporting or opposing the process emerge. The ideal as it has been realized up to that point now faces a crisis of being subjected to public scrutiny and judgment. This may mark a time when the resistance to the process comes to the surface, or when we reconsider what is attainable in the light of what has developed up to this point.

At the opposition, the promise indicated at the conjunction and what we've done to actualize the promise stands on its own in a public way. It always leads to a form of awareness, revealing internal or external factors in the process supporting or resisting what is surfacing.

As I introduced earlier, this begins the second half of the cycle which mirrors the process of the first half of the cycle. The phase from the opposition to the waning square is the first waning quadrant, and features a mirroring of the aspects between the waxing square and the opposition. Because the phase between the opposition and waning square is the process of fulfilling the promise of the seed that sprouted at the conjunction, it involves a "pushing upward" of whatever culminates at the waning square. There is a need to eliminate all that is obstructing or unnecessary to fulfill the process, opening to a larger view and understanding of why things have developed the way they have up to this point.

The culmination of any cycle happens at the waning (upper) square, marking another hemispheric phase shift. At the waning square the process fulfills itself by returning to the hemisphere of "self," opening the doors to the harvest of the purpose of the cycle to be collected between the waning square and coming conjunction. The

158

♄ Saturn: Spiritual Master, Spiritual Friend

harvest takes shape according to the nature of the cycle and the consistency of our efforts as we dealt with the various resistances we encountered, and assistance that came forth, during the phases of how the whole cycle unfolded.

The second waning quadrant from the waning square to the conjunction also mirrors an earlier part of the journey, the span from the original conjunction to the waxing square but in reverse order. However, since the cycle has already been fulfilled and is moving toward completion, this period is about the formation of the seed patterns created throughout the process which will sprout anew at the next conjunction.

DIMENSIONS OF PLANETARY EXPRESSION

Every planet has three levels of expression. Each has its material, or physical level of expression. Each has its social, or emotional level of expression. And each has its spiritual, or philosophical level of expression. Often we find more than one of these operating at the same time, since we are holographic life energy fields, and various parts of our inner and outer life all work together to bring order out of chaos.

We have already explored some different ways a Saturn conjunction to any of our planets might manifest. Let's take a look at how the other aspects might express their energy in the various levels of experience. Obviously, because a waxing square indicates a point of critical emergence, that quality will be present regardless of the level we're looking at.

On the material level, a waxing square would indicate new material conditions, or the need for new ways of acting on emerging material developments. On the social level, the waxing square would mark the point of the emergence of new social skills, new social obligations or conditions, or a new way of experiencing or expressing

159

♄ Saturn: Spiritual Master, Spiritual Friend

feelings. On the spiritual level, the waxing square could indicate the emergence of a new awareness, or a realization that a truth you're expressing must be grounded, as well as tested in the world of others who share or are at odds with the foundations being established.

The opposition always marks a point of repolarization or adjustment to what is emerging in the world. On the material level, an opposition might show the appearance of a form of resistance to the emerging process or aspiration, with the need to test the strength of the resistance in the material world. On a social level, it could demonstrate similarities to the material resistance, such as realizing how social forces will oppose what is coming to the surface. The opposition also offers the possibility of finding complementary energies and people assisting the process, and could mark a point where there is a need to enter into relationships "equal" to the emergent process.

On a spiritual level, an opposition represents a surfacing of the spiritual pulse and a time to find "sacred others" who are part of our larger soul community. This would be a phase when we stand as a spiritual equal with our peers, but also could encounter those who oppose our truth, or those who offer a countering view. The test here is to see how to triangulate the various energies to achieve maximum productivity and understanding within the larger cycle of unfoldment.

Remember that all spiritual differences exist only in the ego mind. As we come to embrace the wisdom revealed to us with every breath we take, we find an ever broader view of the common themes which all spiritual disciplines share, as well as the distinctions within the three great Paths to enlightened awareness. Then the opposition is a challenge to articulate an inclusive understanding, honoring the fact that there are many different paths to enlightenment.

The waning square indicates a time of fulfillment of the process. On the material level, it represents a peak of

♄ Saturn: Spiritual Master, Spiritual Friend

accomplishment based in the quality of the effort up to then, and a time to harvest what can be harvested and prepare for the renewal to come at the next conjunction. At the social-emotional level, the waning square represents a public presentation of the social fulfillment achieved up to that point, and a time to rest easy with how the planetary function is working out through our interpersonal contacts. It is a period of high visibility and/or influence in the public arena, with a need to realize there is nothing left to aspire to in the cycle, but a lot to consolidate as we prepare for the harvest.

At the spiritual level, the waning square represents a time to be at peace with the public presentation or expression of our spiritual awareness and ability to apply the virtues of the planet being squared. It is a time when those parts of our planetary evolution have hit a peak of expression for that cycle, with the subsequent period before the conjunction a time to specialize and refine the essence of those spiritual qualities.

INTRODUCING THE SATURN CYCLE

We'll now examine how the "whole cycle" unfolds as a series of Saturn "pulses" marking long wave periods of mastering our Being. Any Saturn conjunction ends a long term cycle, and initiates a new one. As noted earlier, it takes Saturn about 29 years to move from a conjunction with a point or planet through all the aspects until it comes to the next conjunction. This is why it's important to note what happened and when in the period between the conjunction to the opposition, as it can give us a greater understanding of what to do as it makes all those aspects again, but in reverse order, from the time of the opposition to the next conjunction with that point or planet.

During any Saturn aspect, we may be dealing with something on the material-physical level, the emotional-social level, the mental-spiritual level, or a combination of

♄ Saturn: Spiritual Master, Spiritual Friend

these. In each case, we can express Saturn's powers to use practical methods (Capricorn) coupled with a greater social-aspirational ideal (Aquarius) to utilize our personal power to engineer effective change. And if we can find the structured balance and elegance of Libra in our expression, so much the better!

We know that when Saturn approaches and conjuncts our Ascendant or a planet, we begin to crystalize elements of the coming long term cycle related to our self-awareness or planetary expression. It's a heavy time when we learn the degree to which we have a sense of peace about our destiny, or experience life or those parts of our personality as a burdensome and dreary slog. It all depends on our attitude and willingness to accept the reality of what is, and could be, changing what we can change and accepting what we cannot.

As we've discussed, Saturn conjunct the Ascendant always brings a new learning rigor, a more responsible role to play in our world, or some more important duty to be performed. As Saturn continues on its journey and moves into and occupies each subsequent house (the 2nd, 3rd, 4th, and so on around the chart wheel), those parts of life are restructured into our larger organic wholeness.

As it transits each sector, we learn new responses to the inherent limitations and evolutionary necessities in those circumstances. These two+ year-periods are when we learn to demonstrate diligent and responsible attitudes about those things we must accept to find a greater security in our self-expression and sense of competency in those life areas.

Each house it moves through brings us opportunities to mature and become more clear and deliberate in our approach to fulfilling karma and Dharma in those areas of life. This allows us to exercise some command over our evolution in the life areas indicated by each house. As Saturn moves through each house, we learn every ending is followed by a new beginning. Even as Saturn shuts some doors, others are opened.

♄ Saturn: Spiritual Master, Spiritual Friend

When Saturn conjuncts, squares, or opposes a planet or our Ascendant, to the degree we have not made Saturn our friend, it manifests as negative Saturn experiences of feeling depressed, oppressed, repressed, limited, frustrated, and "saturnine." These are crucial life points where we deal with Saturn's sobering influence, and must demonstrate Saturn's virtues. We certainly confront a need to "keep it real," and must accept hard truths about our inner head and heart space, as well as our outer life affairs.

These hard Saturn aspects may bring feelings of being "stuck" or we may confront resistance to who we are and what we're doing, allowing us to evaluate the methods at our disposal, and make corrective adjustments to bring our process back into alignment with the best ideal we can achieve.

When we're feeling "stuck," it's merely the result of not moving, or feeling a lack of movement. If this feeling is associated with fear, it means we have fallen into a useless illusion. If "feeling stuck" brings a sense of depression, it indicates something from the subconscious mind is trying to surface. When we take a hard look (Saturn) at those things we're "depressing," we gain power through overcoming the sources of anxiety or apprehension through "naming the demon." This is a technique of stripping power from all we fear.

Difficult feelings come up when we've hit critical turning points in our long and short term evolution. The timing on when they happen give us clues about when they began, what they're associated with, and how to implement a more healthy set of patterns. Each challenging Saturn transit reveals to us what we chose and when we chose it, if we track the cause back to the source. Then we can examine why we chose it, and whether it has served its purpose. Is something we're struggling with a product of our actions or our inactions? Is the struggle a result of a failure in the plan, or just that "things have changed?" Is this crisis showing us something we've neglected and must tend to, or is it showing us something

℞ Saturn: Spiritual Master, Spiritual Friend

is over and done?

When we confront questions of this nature, we know something has changed, and something needs to change. The task is to turn ineffective responses to more productive responses, finding ways to express these in the material, social-emotional, and psychological-spiritual affairs of our lives. In such cases a good attitude helps us through our crises of re-integration.

Ultimately, the answer to every difficult transit is "What are we going to do about it?" Since all answers to all problems are found on the spiritual planes of existence, then we must go there to find the best response to any challenge. This is where a spiritual discipline helps, since it gives us a reference point to access our wisdom and universal wisdom. As we make Saturn our friend, over time we more easily detach from ego-mind and its assumptions, and find the perfect ways, means, and times to go into a deeper connection with All-That-Is, regardless of the aspects being made in our charts.

SATURN WAXING SQUARE THE ASCENDANT AND NATAL PLANETS

Saturn makes a waxing square, or emergent (lower) square about seven years after the conjunction. This period offers us the first big turning point in the cycle of unfoldment, and features important new developments as well as opportunities to correct the focus and trajectory of the process. The lower square to the Ascendant may entail grounding our emergent sense of self or the new role or discipline which began at the conjunction.

A waxing square challenges us to take responsibility for the structure of the foundation of whatever the cycle is about, and change what needs changing. There may be new starts, or significant breaks from the past. This is a mid-course correction period, and often accompanies the need to revise memories of the

164

♄ Saturn: Spiritual Master, Spiritual Friend

past and cut loose of patterns keeping us hindered by obsolete fears, duties, or assumptions. It may be a time where we turn a corner, or put the brakes on an old pattern that no longer works and turn our energies to more beneficial and effective methods.

This time of long term restructuring of our foundations may bring tension, especially if we want things to develop any faster than they are unfolding. It's a very important time, since "as the roots, so the flowers." After the lower square, we have the platform for future successes.

Saturn's lower square to the planets represents a shift in how we will choose to express those planetary energies in the future. It marks a reality check on how we are or are not authentically living new forms of experience which began when Saturn conjuncted those planets. The waxing square allows us new forms of self-discovery, reorientation, and gives us a sense of the long term building plan which will continue after the square.

Saturn waxing square any planet marks a point where we must accept what is emerging, correct what needs correcting, and be patient as we navigate the major changes accompanying these periods. Because it marks a point of "critical emergence" of the planetary function, it shows us both our expertise as well as the blockages assisting us to focus our power in the next phase between the waxing square and the opposition.

SATURN OPPOSITION THE ASCENDANT AND NATAL PLANETS

Saturn's opposition to our Ascendant happens about 14-15 years after the conjunction, and is a time when the world responds to our self-definition in some clear ways. At that point, things are surfacing which will affect our lives for years to come, requiring we leave other things behind and become a true equal in our relationship

♄ Saturn: Spiritual Master, Spiritual Friend

to the world and the other people in our life.

Saturn opposing the Ascendant is a time to get beyond controlling or being controlled in relationships, or blaming others for our limitations. It begins a period of getting clear about boundaries and expressing a maturity in all relationships, and may accompany a sense of wanting relationships with others who are more mature.

By the opposition we've been prepared for a greater effectiveness, and this point ushers in approximately 14 years of fulfilling the promise of the seed forms set into motion at the conjunction. Based in what we've learned, we may be offered opportunities which could involve playing a more important or substantial role in our world, or find ways to be more structured in doing those things we still have to do to fulfill our evolved sense of Self.

As we discussed, when Saturn opposes a planet, it indicates a surfacing of something the planet symbolizes. It may lead to an understanding of the gap between the reality and the ideal in a facet of our personality, or it can manifest as someone symbolized by that planet coming into or leaving our life. This period is frequently accompanied by oppositions or polarizations in our lives teaching us how to make progress despite feeling like there's an unyielding resistance or a dead weight in areas associated with the planet being opposed.

For example, when Saturn opposes our Sun, we get to examine and let go of all that would inhibit our Light/Life, and break loose from old control systems. It often accompanies leaving behind lesser duties and responsibilities and taking on more important ones. We get clear about the limits of our realm, and anything that opposes our Light.

Saturn shows us when we must let go of the remains of the past we no longer need. Because the oppositions can work out through people and circumstances which make us more aware of what opposes us, and what supports us, it's a time to take a new look at who supports our efforts, and who is an obstacle to

℞ Saturn: Spiritual Master, Spiritual Friend

our efforts. During oppositions, if we encounter difficulties in relationships, it's usually because we or they are operating off of useless or oppressive limitations and restrictions. When Saturn opposes the Sun, we look at our control issues. Those who are trying to impose their sense of order or control on us will often find we are resistant or antagonistic to that control, or if we're trying to impose our sense of order or control on another, we may experience antagonism or resistance to our efforts.

It is a time to stop useless pushing and wheel spinning, and accept the protocol or methods which will ensure the eventual fulfillment of the purpose of the cycle. Examine any internal resistance to the changes presenting themselves during these time spans, and find an objective view which will yield a greater understanding of what's going on and why.

When confronted by oppositions from Saturn, examine all you're dealing with or struggling with. If something has become burdensome, stifling, or restrictive, then it's time to re-evaluate the part that thing or behavior plays in your life. Is it really what you believe in, what you are dedicated to, and gives you a sense of being in command of your life, or are you playing to someone else's agenda, whether present or from your past? Are you living the life and relationships you want, or trying to conform to someone else's rules? Either way this represents a period where we define our purpose more clearly and get ready to bring things to culmination over the next seven years which follow.

SATURN WANING SQUARE THE ASCENDANT AND NATAL PLANETS

Saturn makes a waning square, or culminating (upper) square, to our Ascendant about 21-22 years after the initial conjunction, and brings the fulfillment to our labor of redefining our purpose on our own terms relative to the

167

℞ Saturn: Spiritual Master, Spiritual Friend

world we're in. Sometimes it brings widespread recognition and power or greater influence, if these were our intention and purpose, and we did what we had to do to embrace a more important role to play in the world. This crystallizes our public persona in some way and fulfills an old self-image.

This is a time to be a wise administrator, preparing to turn inward after the harvest time following this culmination. It always brings a high degree of visibility within our chosen sphere of influence. The waning square to the Ascendant is a time to relax into our public role and enjoy doing our duty. There may be professional challenges indicating some things are done, allowing us to shift our methods and move in new directions.

Saturn upper square a planet shows the process of growth which started about 22 years before has now reached an apex, and we must learn how to turn with the changing emphasis. This marks a time of fulfilled expression of the planet it squares, and is a point where we must turn the planetary expression to different ends. This matures parts of our personality so we'll have the skills we need in the next cycle beginning at the coming conjunction.

At Saturn's upper square to a natal planet, we must see how to reorient toward new forms of expression more appropriate to our advanced evolution after over two decades of growth and maturation of those planetary functions. It's a time to conserve energy and not prolong exhausting conflicts.

Like the waxing square, Saturn's waning square to a planet marks the turning of a corner or a time when we put the brakes on old patterns which have fulfilled their purpose in our life. The seven to eight years after the upper square is a harvest period, where we complete our understanding of what the long cycle was about, and how it revealed elements of Dharma as we fulfilled karmic patterns through choices we made at each turn of the wheel.

♄ Saturn: Spiritual Master, Spiritual Friend

* * * * * * * * *

As Saturn transits all of our planets, making conjunctions, squares, oppositions, and all the other aspects, we deepen, mature, and reshape those things we need to in order to become a better, more effective participant in the world. Any difficulties, struggles, or frustrations we encounter during these times are clear signals of a need to change our methods and responses to those problems. Saturn transits help us redefine all the parts of ourselves and our purpose as we learn to eliminate our fears and those things which inhibit the expression of our spiritual values.

A good way to describe Saturn's friction is like a burnishing from a grinder smoothing a surface. With time and patience, Saturn can help level things, even things, polish things, and make them aesthetically pleasing as per its exaltation in Libra. Over time, a healthy Saturn makes all things pleasing through a balanced sense of proportion.

After Saturn touches any part of our being, we are to some degree more serious or clear-minded, whether pessimistically or optimistically. When Saturn visits a planet or house we are definitely more sober about those parts of life symbolized by the house or planet. We are taught what we can live with or cannot, what we will or will not tolerate, in terms of what the planets symbolize in our lives, whether personality, people, purpose, or process.

This brings us back to the value of limitations in showing us the areas of self and life we are mastering, as well as those things we still have yet to master. When we learn to respond to Saturn's various conjunctions, squares, and oppositions as spiritual adults, we make each limitation the means to transcend that limitation, and accept our need to master all which confronts us before entering into larger fields of learning and practice.

Here a quote from the great Arhat Paul Foster Case seems appropriate: "Right interpretation of the

℞ Saturn: Spiritual Master, Spiritual Friend

necessity for limitation in any form of manifested existence is the secret of dominion. Wrong interpretation of the same thing is the cause of our slavery to conditions. The clue to the right understanding is the aphorism, 'He who would rule Nature must first obey her laws.' " *

As it makes all the aspects with all our planets, Saturn transits teach us when we must re-shape how each planetary personality function manifests. Saturn is how we Spirit/Souls learn to manage our bodies, feelings, and ideas. Through the ever-renewing patience, perseverance, and maturity Saturn offers us in each chapter of life, we can find a fair, balanced, and reasoned out well-rounded perspective. Then through conscious choices we demonstrate our spiritual virtues as we need to, and can become the living manifestation of the intelligent Light of Love to others.

TRANSITING SATURN AS AN EVOLVING PROCESS

As Saturn moves through the various signs, it ends and begins things associated with those signs. As it moves through subsequent signs, it ends and begins things associated with those subsequent signs, and further develops the things set into motion in previous transits. This section takes a brief look at some specific examples of how Saturn's long-wave transits and aspects can work. We'll begin with what's been going on in recent years.

Those who have a planet in the early degrees of a Cardinal sign (Aries, Cancer, Libra, Capricorn), were exposed to a restructuring of those planetary energies in late 2009 and early 2010 via Saturn in Libra making a conjunction, square, or opposition to planets in the early degrees of those signs. This group reviewed things during the time Saturn was retrograde, and when it moved forward again in the Summer of 2010 it made those aspects a third time. Then those Saturn lessons were

170

♄ Saturn: Spiritual Master, Spiritual Friend

finished, and a new way of expressing the energies of the planets Saturn aspected was launched.

It moved forward into the middle and late degrees of Libra between late 2010 and late 2012, and brought Saturn lessons involving beginnings (conjunction), emergent responsibilities (waxing square), new rises (opposition), and culminations (waning square) to people with planets in the middle and late degrees of Aries, Cancer, Libra, and Capricorn. Then from October 2012 through October 2013, it moved into the early degrees of Scorpio, bringing those same lessons to all with planets in the early degrees of the Fixed signs (Taurus, Leo, Scorpio, Aquarius).

However, even though Saturn entered the Fixed sign of Scorpio, people with planets in the Cardinal signs continued to be affected by those previous conjunctions, squares, and oppositions, even though they occurred in the past. This group continued to develop the pulses set into motion when Saturn was in Libra, while dealing with another set of lessons triggered by Saturn in Scorpio. So even though Saturn subsequently made other aspects to those planets in the early degrees of Aries, Cancer, Libra, or Capricorn, the lessons of Saturn in Libra which came up between 2009 and 2012 set patterns related to how those planetary functions would express into the future, and changed as aspects were made to those early degree planets.

This demonstrates the continuum of our experiences over time revealing how to apply our planetary functions expertly. Long after an initial aspect is made, even though different aspects occur after that, each phase is merely the next step in a process of how a planetary function greets or resists another planet's influence.

Saturn in Scorpio between 2012-2015 brought different lessons to those with planets in Aries, Cancer, Libra, and Capricorn through a variety of aspects made to the earlier conjunctions, squares, and oppositions. At the same time, Saturn in Scorpio brought conjunctions, squares, and oppositions to planets in Taurus, Leo,

Saturn: Spiritual Master, Spiritual Friend

Scorpio, and Aquarius.

Saturn in Sagittarius, 2015-2017, makes conjunctions, squares, or oppositions to planets in Gemini, Virgo, Sagittarius, and Pisces, while making aspects marking the next stages of unfoldment involving planets it aspected in the previous Cardinal and Fixed sign transits.

Saturn is in Capricorn from 2018-2020, where it again makes conjunctions, squares, and oppositions to planets in Aries, Cancer, Libra, and Capricorn. Though it's a definite turning point for anything that came forth during Saturn in Libra, it simultaneously moves the evolution of all our Fixed and Mutable planetary expressions to yet another step and another set of lessons.

Saturn is in Aquarius from 2020-2023, where it again makes conjunctions, squares, and oppositions to planets in Taurus, Leo, Scorpio, and Aquarius. This is a turning point (waxing square) for whatever began at the previous transit of Saturn in Scorpio, and represents a time of stable expression for the beginnings initiated during Saturn in Libra as well as a productive time for the beginnings initiated during Saturn in Sagittarius.

Saturn is in Pisces from 2024-2026, where it again makes conjunctions, squares, and oppositions to planets in Gemini, Virgo, Sagittarius, and Pisces. This is the turning point for what began with Saturn in Sagittarius, and is a time of stable expression for the beginnings initiated during Saturn in Scorpio. As it also finishes the waxing hemicycle for what began with Saturn in Libra, it is easy to see how there are many different Saturn cycles, each in a different phase of restructuring our various planetary energies and departments of life.

Using my table of Saturn positions in the signs in Chapter Seven, you should be able to do rough calculations and see when it will make various conjunctions, squares, oppositions, as well as sextiles and trines to various planets in your charts, A more detailed and exact timing will be found by consulting an ephemeris.

♄ Saturn: Spiritual Master, Spiritual Friend

Saturn makes a conjunction, square, or opposition to Ascendant, Sun or planets in:	
Saturn in Libra Late 2009 - 2012	Aries, Cancer, Libra, Capricorn
Saturn in Scorpio 2012 - 2015	Taurus, Leo, Scorpio, Aquarius
Saturn in Sagittarius 2015 - 2017	Gemini, Virgo Sagittarius, Pisces
Saturn in Capricorn 2018 - 2020	Aries, Cancer, Libra Capricorn
Saturn in Aquarius 2020 - 2023	Taurus, Leo, Scorpio, Aquarius
Saturn in Pisces 2024 - 2026	Gemini, Virgo, Sagittarius, Pisces

♄ Saturn: Spiritual Master, Spiritual Friend

CHAPTER 8

THE SATURN RETURN

We now turn our attention to one of the most important and life altering transits of all, the Saturn return. The Saturn return is when transiting Saturn returns to its natal position. It always occurs between the age of 27 and 29, and again between 57 and 59, and for those who are fortunate to live a very long life, between 85 and 89.

These are times of serious realizations which alter the trajectory of our life, marking "points of no return" when lesser things must be set aside, and we confront fundamental truths related to our past, present, and future. A Saturn return always begins well before the actual contact, seems to last a lot longer than we would like, and generally speaking is one of the most dreaded and misunderstood points in personal evolution.

It is usually a difficult period with a lot of stress, pressure, and hard choices. Important parts of the life come to an end, sobering realizations are faced, and the weight of the world is felt, very acutely. Saturn returns are when one of two things happen; either we relax into the authority, responsibilities, and recognition we have, executing our duties secure in who we are and what we've accomplished, or we realize we must turn away from things which are fulfilled (whether we want to or not) and accept the promise of finding a greater wisdom, as well as and more effective and satisfying ways of living.

During the Saturn return, we come to see how much free will we have to choose positive Self-empowering responses in the face of hard realities and the end of

℞ Saturn: Spiritual Master, Spiritual Friend

something which has been a major part of learning our life purpose. Often it accompanies a significant birth or death, a change or loss of job, an important job promotion, a major move, a sense of having no control over life, a chronic condition becomes evident, we graduate into a new life, or retire from an old life (and sometimes more than one of these!) If a Saturn return brings us face to face with any of these events, we confront the culmination of an old way of living and the beginning of a new era, and must accept that some things are no more.

Saturn returns are most difficult for those who have resisted or are resisting their own tide of personal evolution, and are times to deal with whatever is creating a sense of frustration, struggle, or meaninglessness. Whether difficult, easy, or simply the passing of a baton as one era ends and another begins, it's a time to find the psychological skills to use during the transition which can open us to a more fulfilling life in the years to come. During this time of clearing out old psychological refuse, whatever must change *will* change, whether we want it to or not, and whether we like it or not.

While we realize something is over and done, we often don't know how it happened, with no idea or ability to continue what was, or recapture it in any way. Time and experience have brought us to the limit of our previous ambitions, and as we examine our priorities, we know we must drop everything we no longer have the time or energy to pursue.

If we confront a lack or deficiency at a Saturn return or burdensome external or internal struggles, we are challenged to see what we need to cultivate in our long term "enlightened self-interest," and let go self-defeating attitudes and behaviors. Through the finality of what we're going through, we see the futility of clutching at old forms of thinking and feeling, and can get clear about how we can chart a better life course.

So what good comes out of a Saturn return? We learn two big things at a Saturn return: 1) We have absolutely no control over anyone else's behavior, and 2)

♄ Saturn: Spiritual Master, Spiritual Friend

Nothing "out there" matters more than our ability to choose our reactions to events, and how we will handle them. We realize we are not responsible for how other people choose to behave, and have no power to make them "do the right thing." How we respond to that realization creates conflict and struggle, or an acceptance that we can only choose for ourselves and not another.

Whether the first or second Saturn return, we find applying our free will works in very powerful ways. We are offered a chance to renew our lives by embracing a new maturity and sense of purpose, setting aside old attitudes and opening to a new long term adventure in living a more purposeful life on our own terms. The power and sense of security with who we are and what we could achieve in the future empowers us to live life the way we want, unbound from many previous obligations that no longer matter.

However, that doesn't mean we can simply do what we want. Again, if something is not true for us, or if a prior potential in something we have been doing is fulfilled and there's nothing significant for us to learn along those lines, then regardless of our best efforts trying to "push the river," we will not achieve satisfying results.

Before the first Saturn return, many values and assumptions we held as "set in stone" were encoded into our consciousness via the ego-mind by elders, generating patterns of conscious and unconscious responses to the collective values of our societal and cultural matrix. These became life patterns and rules we lived by. At the first Saturn return, we find many values and assumptions are no longer true for us, and leave behind those which are frustrating so we can feel like we're getting back on course, even if that course is radically different than the one we were on before the Saturn return. While parts of our experience may feel like we've just survived a train wreck, we also know there's nothing we can do but walk on.

By taking an inventory of what we accepted and avoided in earlier years, we can move out of unconscious patterns and obsolete conceptions of who we are into more deliberate and thoughtful expressions of our hearts.

♄ Saturn: Spiritual Master, Spiritual Friend

By letting go of internal blockages and embracing a new way pursuing a deeper and richer life, we feel the joy of being alive, steering our personality toward our destiny, with no fear of unknown experiences to come.

I have found the Saturn return influence begins when it first enters the sign Saturn is in, as well as when it comes to within about ten degrees of Saturn if it's in another sign. For example, my Saturn is in the 29th degree of Virgo at the very end of that sign. And yet I remember feeling its influence the day it entered Virgo in September 2007, even though it was still 28 degrees away from an exact conjunction to my Saturn.

My exact Saturn return happened two years later in October 2009. Saturn then entered Libra, and then retrograded back over my Saturn in May 2010, finally going stationary direct at 28 Virgo. After that, it crossed back over the exact degree and minute of my Saturn in June 2010, and remained within orb through September. In my experience, my second Saturn return lasted for about three years!! And yes, my life was radically restructured, and the person I was by September 2010 was radically different than the person I had been in the Summer of 2007.

My sense of responsibility was different, my sense of purpose was different, what I could tolerate was different, the roles I was willing to play were different, with the critical factor being *I chose my path every step of the way*. I knew I confronted the end of an old way of life, and needed to open to a newer, more fulfilling future. When I tried to hold on to inert or sclerotic responses, I felt the weight of my life as a burdensome tiring slog.

Both of my Saturn returns brought a full stop to old attitudes and assumptions holding me back. Both periods helped me to choose a new identity and the power of my determination to chart a new course, with major breaks from stagnant systems and people. Each time I turned away from life patterns which had run their course and people who had become abusive, leaving behind my old life and any sense of obligation about tolerating hurtful behaviors from others. I found I just didn't have the time or

177

♄ Saturn: Spiritual Master, Spiritual Friend

inclination to invite or indulge some things I did before my Saturn return. While each brought devastating losses, they also helped me to see my strengths as well as my ability to live more autonomously.

Again, Saturn does not "make us" be a certain way; it's more like our inner Saturn function finally realizes, as a result of time and the fulfillment of Dharma, that some things just can't be done any more. The Saturn return helps us remember we are the engineers of our own lives, the determiners of our fate through how we apply free will, and the dispensers of "glory or gloom" to ourselves, and no others.

Nothing external has the power to override our ability to decide what we will and will not do with our lives. We can always choose to transcend the lower nature and the traps of imperfect personality expressions. Though external events may factor into how we manifest our destiny, we always have the power to decide how we will and will not act, and replace habits of the lower nature with more consciously chosen higher responses.

Since character is destiny, as we make our character we make our destiny. Saturn cycles merely demonstrate the timing when parts of our inner nature must learn certain lessons as a direct result of the maturation process, and get clear about the cause-and-effect cycles we set into motion before these periods of radical confrontations, realizations, choices, changes, and decisions.

A Saturn return offers us opportunities to leave behind guilt, blame, and regret for all that has been and all that hasn't. It's a great time to throw off psychological burdens, and come to a new resolve to live a better life. For me, I found time and maturity had brought me face to face with my ability to be at peace in my own realm without worrying about what others thought, and I embraced trusting the wisdom I had accumulated through many years of direct experience. I found it became relatively easy to be at peace with my ways of living my life, which led me to a genuine long term renewal through accepting more

♄ Saturn: Spiritual Master, Spiritual Friend

fulfilling ways to be a spiritual adult, with an expanded ability to shine my spiritual Light and truth in the world.

The Saturn return is usually not a "joyous" or easy time, since everything seems very heavy due to what comes and goes. However, If we find the right point of view, we can come to a sense of calm confidence by keeping in mind we are moving toward a better way of living, embracing new roles appropriate to our wisdom, enabling us to enjoy the future as a grand adventure of being a Spirit in the material world.

Saturn helps us know when to move on, in an absolute sense. We understand the value of time as a dimension of evolution, and begin to understand how each step we take becomes the foundation for the next step, so Dharma unfolds in perfect form.

Ultimately, through Saturn we can rediscover our primal innocence, where we do what's right for the greatest good for all, without ulterior motives or the need to revert to controlling behaviors. We just have to learn to be wise in our understanding without being "old." This is the understanding we've accumulated from life experiences teaching us universal lessons of the human condition.

Age teaches us humility, acceptance, patience, and discernment about the best use of time and energy. With the perfection of our Saturn function, we become part of the wisdom of our ancestry, our era, and the holographic patterns of all who share our life lessons. We become the gatekeepers, the custodians of the wisdom we have learned, the referees in the game of Life in our areas of expertise.

Saturn lessons help us learn and demonstrate a greater way for others who accompany or follow us in the areas of the Ageless Wisdom we share. Everything we must go through points the way to embrace Saturn's higher qualities as efficient means to move through experiences leading us to become greater than we could have imagined.

As we grow during all the Saturn conjunctions, squares, and oppositions to its natal position, we acquire

179

♄ Saturn: Spiritual Master, Spiritual Friend

fundamental knowledge about how well we're handling Saturn and every other part of our personality. All of these phases guide us through many different kinds of changes culminating at the Saturn return. Each turning point after that momentous occasion gives us the practice yielding the keys to the perfection of our inner Saturn function.

As we learn to cope with issues and necessities when Saturn conjuncts, squares, and opposes natal Saturn, we learn lessons which will last for the rest of our lives. The points where Saturn squares and opposes its natal position are periods when we adjust the trajectory of our lives, bringing our affairs into a more perfect alignment with our higher purpose.

THE SECOND SATURN RETURN

Saturn again returns to its birth place again between 57 and 59. This is the second Saturn return, where we choose once again how we want to live, this time for what most of us believe will be the rest of our productive years. Having fulfilled (for better or worse) the course we set at the first Saturn return, we are again forced by circumstances to turn away from old assumptions while turning to a new way of living our Truth of Being.

While the first Saturn return occurs when we believe we still have infinite possibilities, by the second Saturn return we are harvesting the fruits of our labors. Many things we once aspired to are complete, and we also are clear about what we cannot change. At the second Saturn return, we can claim the wisdom born of life experiences we've had since the first Saturn return through distilling the deeper and higher truths from the realizations we've had so far, reflected through the filter of over 30 years of adult experience.

We cannot ignore certain realities at the second Saturn return, since we get clear about those things which

℞ Saturn: Spiritual Master, Spiritual Friend

no longer work for us and can embrace newer, more appropriate forms of expressing our evolved authentic Self. We come to sobering realizations about the trajectory of our life and reflect on the many paths we've taken to get to that point. The more a Being attempts to deviate from the destiny already set into motion between the first and second Saturn return, the greater the struggle and frustration.

A sense of world weariness is felt at the second Saturn return. We know there are fewer days ahead of us than behind us, and know our limitations. We know what we care about, as well as what we don't want to deal with any more. We know life is not as it was and never will be again, and we know we're not getting any younger.

Since we've already gone through just about every emotion a human can experience during the two previous Lunar returns preceding the second Saturn return, we also know a certain type of "emotional exhaustion" since there is no attachment to investing in prior emotional states we've already been through. We learn how to accept the timing on things without getting stuck in thinking something is supposed to look a certain way.

A primary requirement of the late 50s is to accept who we are and the destiny we're living, and not get lost in images of who we never were and a destiny not ours to live. Age has brought us perspective through experience. Things we cannot conceive of when younger come under consideration with age. We see everything we've longed for as an idea within a larger perspective of what we put energy into and accomplished, or didn't.

We're no longer just cruising through our 40s or even the "confident transitions" of the early 50s. As we approach the second Saturn return, we find we no longer can muster the energy to try to accomplish "great things." We confront mortality and physical limitations, but it doesn't mean we feel that life is done. It's more like we know a way of seeing things is over. We come to understand some things are not for us to do, since if they were, we would have already done them. That's why we

181

must find a new way to enjoy life while leaving a lot behind, since we realize we no longer yearn for those things of youth, and no longer consider options we may have in our 30s and 40s.

When we were younger, we were unaware of many things due to a lack of experience. Since we had no larger frame of reference, we embraced many ideas, feelings, and actions thinking "it seemed like a good idea at the time." Then we found we could pursue certain vectors of growth to an almost infinite degree, but also encountered blockages in other things we tried to do.

As we actualized certain potentials, we also came to understand the natural organic limits in how much we could achieve, and simultaneously came to understand there were certain things we would never accomplish because they were contrary to our true nature, and/or were diverting us from the path to spiritual maturity. At the second Saturn return, we can understand why it was beneficial for us to be limited in some ways, and in accepting what we are to do in the next life chapter we can focus energy effectively, and find peace and fulfillment within those natural limits.

The second Saturn return is usually hardest on those who still operate out of immaturity, irresponsibility, frustrated ambitions, unrealized desires, or fear. It always presents major challenges for those who have not learned to embrace their destiny with joy, or ignored the physical or emotional lessons in the critical turning points between 29 and 58. It is very difficult for people who want to continue doing things which are already fulfilled and done. Those who cling to rules, assumptions, and unfulfilling behaviors left over from younger days will feel frustration about things not turning out as expected, or the sense that something external prevented or is preventing them from living a better life.

Over the years, I've also observed every single person experiencing their second Saturn return was forced to slow down because they realized they just didn't have the strength or stamina they had in their 30s and 40s, and were tired of pushing to accomplish more and more. It's a time when we do have a conscious sense of being older, and it becomes increasingly harder to ignore the physical limitations we are living with as a result of the aging process. Because we don't have the strength to pursue things we used to, we come to accept that win, lose, or draw, an old set of life interests is over, whether we think they're done or not.

Saturn returns often accompany the realization that we have not examined certain things in life which now demand consideration. At the second Saturn return we are offered opportunities to reflect on "the unexamined life," and how things came to be the way they are. We review our lives, and ask ourselves why we did certain things and not others. We can reflect on critical choices which affected the trajectory of life events, and see how each of them made a difference in how our lives unfolded after that.

Sometimes the second Saturn return brings regrets for what we did, or what we didn't do. There can be questions about the roads not taken, but again, we do not know they would have turned out as we assume. We never know the confluence of events which could result from current choices based in assumptions which may not be valid if we chose otherwise. We can only assume that our life choices creating our experiences were the ones we needed to fulfill Dharma within the Ring Pass Not at each critical junction in life.

Those who chose to embrace the quest to find a more satisfying and effective expression of their purpose on Earth before or during the first Saturn return and then lived their truth and integrity the best they were able in their 30s, 40s, and early 50s find the second Saturn return makes it clear they have lived the life they were supposed to live. It always marks a point where we know the next act in the play of our life has been fulfilled, and opens the gates so we may embrace a new adventure, since we're at the end of the course we set in our late 20s.

♄ Saturn: Spiritual Master, Spiritual Friend

How we respond to the second Saturn return is the difference between being a grumpy old person and one who is full of life even in the season of the silver hair. If we willingly embrace a new role to play, and accept that we can find great fulfillment within the natural limits of age, we can experience enormous contentment in knowing who we are, what we're here to do, and express joyous, natural, and organic forms of our loving wise intelligence.

I figure the third Saturn return is when we become exempt from most of what we had to learn in earlier Saturn periods, since by the time we hit 87-88, either we have it mastered or we haven't. I would think being at peace with our wisdom and our experience, finding ways our lives "furthered the Great Work," is about all there is to do. And have fun, of course!!

THE SECOND SATURN RETURN ALSO BRINGS US A JUPITER RETURN

The second Saturn is a special event for another reason. It is something experienced by everyone who lives to be 60. Around the age of 58-60, every one of us has our second Saturn return, and around the same time, our fifth Jupiter return. Usually there's a time gap between the two, and seldom do the two occupy the same transiting degrees at the same time as they did at birth.

At various points in time throughout life, all the planets return to their natal positions based in the length of their orbit, bringing a renewal of the planetary energy for another cycle. This resets the larger pulses of evolution in our life relative to each planet, with the influence working out through the houses and other planets they influence.

There are Lunar returns, Solar returns, Mercury returns, Venus returns, and Mars returns, as well as Jupiter and Saturn returns. Each gives us a long range snapshot of the changes in that planetary function within us over the following months or years. Uranus returns

184

♄ Saturn: Spiritual Master, Spiritual Friend

happen once in 84 years, so they are the least frequent return we humans can experience. No one except very advanced Rishis and other spiritual Beings experience a Neptune or Pluto return.

A Jupiter return brings opportunities to renew and refresh our Jupiterian qualities. Whether of adventure, abundance, compassion, extravagance, new truths, new belief systems, a new understanding of a larger view of life, or a broader, freer self-expression or higher awareness, it's the end of a 11 to 12 year period and the beginning of another.

A Jupiter return can bring us liberation, new life openings, and visions of greater possibilities. This is why it's a very important event. Every 11 to 12 years we naturally open to a new sense of a greater vision and greater possibilities, as well as ways to expand our life and broaden our understanding of what we believe to be true. As with all planetary cycles, we can figure out a lot of what's happening and why related to our Jupiter evolution by looking at our last Jupiter return, and examining the points where Jupiter made an upper or lower square or opposition to our natal Jupiter.

Even though Jupiter returns to its natal position several times before our second Saturn return, we only experience a Jupiter return and a Saturn return at the same time during the second Saturn return. It marks a time when the second return of our experiential wisdom meets the fifth return of our openness to growing into a broader view of our potential, as well as a deeper compassionate view of the human experience.

A Jupiter return opens our imagination and renews an expanded vision of greater opportunities, and a Saturn return brings us completion, maturity, and a sense of finality about how we have lived life through triumphs and tragedies. When these two returns occur at the same time, it sets up an interesting dynamic for the rest of our life. One is expansion; one is contraction. One opens, the other limits. One represents our spiritual, moral, and ethical sense, while the other represents our ambition and ability

♄ Saturn: Spiritual Master, Spiritual Friend

to chart our course through thick and thin.

The Jupiter returns bring us one form of renewal, while the Saturn returns bring another type of renewal. Of the two, Saturn has a longer wave and a slower pace. It makes clear how we have lived our purpose to our own ends or not, selfishly or not, responsibly or not. And it always holds the promise of a renewed sense of purpose and a greater peace of mind when we cast off attitudes keeping us boxed in by echoes of old perceptions and claim the power to embrace the fullness of our destiny.

So the Jupiter return ends old truths and futures while opening new visions and new adventures, while the Saturn return most definitely shuts doors and opens others. However, as I mentioned earlier in this work, because Jupiter's orbit is inside Saturn's, our Jupiter possibilities are bound by our Saturn response. At the second Saturn return, by how we experience life, whether as a tiring struggle or a turn to more fulfilling things which truly matter to us, we are shown the degree we've made Saturn our friend.

If our Saturn is functioning in a healthy way, and we have embraced its virtues and turned away from childish things at critical moments, we know a mature power to shape destiny through wise choices. When we are clear about our limitations as well as how and when we can transcend them, we become clear about how to do our thing in our way without fear or feeling like life has lost its luster.

When we experience our fifth Jupiter return and our second Saturn return between 59-60, it's hello and goodbye, yes and no, present and past, made obvious by outer events demonstrating elements of our entire life as we have experienced both Jupiterian and Saturnian energies. It's a strange time to be sure, and points the way to a greater personal fulfillment in the twilight season of our life on Earth.

♄ Saturn: Spiritual Master, Spiritual Friend

* * * * * * * *

With increased longevity beyond previous generations comes the opportunity to live a life unknown to centuries of people who came before us. If the fundamental human quest is for meaning and purpose in this fleeting existence, then that quest does not end nearly as soon as it used to. Many on Earth now live into their 80s and 90s, and are still alert and awake enough to want to enjoy the time they still have. And so the quest continues.

How does one find a sense of significance in the twilight years? How do we find purpose and meaning in the last years of our life on Earth? The answer is found in how we respond to the singular life event of the time span when Jupiter and Saturn return to their natal positions. At that point we "check in" with where we are at in the moment relative to where we began our Jupiter-Saturn journey at birth, and are offered a renewal lasting the rest of this life and beyond.

While the period beyond the second Saturn return holds limitations unknown to younger people, the promise of great joy and fulfillment are offered to those who wholeheartedly accept the fact that they have complete power to be as they need to be, freed from any sense that the past binds us to old rules. After 60, we are free to be who we are without allowing the world's opinions to strip us of the power to speak our truth and live our authenticity, because that power is anchored in our age, experience, and understanding.

From that point on, we are freed to live our Higher Self in countless ways, giving and receiving as much love as we can. While there is always a sense of what is dead and gone, never to return, there is also a rich vein of experience to mine which will yield countless insights and gems of wisdom that have meaning because we have lived those experiences. We are all on a quest for meaning. We can catch glimpses of what we are supposed to understand about this life by reflecting on all we've been

187

♄ Saturn: Spiritual Master, Spiritual Friend

through, and seeing how we grew, whether the easy way or the hard way.

The second Saturn return gives us an opportunity to examine our life track, and claim our wisdom. The fifth Jupiter return gives us the "quintessence" of our Jupiter, where we are offered the opportunity to examine our Jupiterian experiences across vast cycles of time and can synthesize them into glimpses of the perfected jewel our life actually is. We are the raw specimen, we are the stonecutter, and when the cutting and polishing process is complete, we are the perfected jewel after each life of striving.

♄ Saturn: Spiritual Master, Spiritual Friend

CHAPTER 9
THE PROGRESSED MOON
THE SATURN CYCLE
AND CRITICAL LIFE CHOICES

As I introduced in Chapter One, the progressed Moon and transiting Saturn and how their cycles relate to each other are extremely important pulses marking critical points of major emotional change related to our maturing sense of self. After we are born, our progressed Moon moves through all the signs, and returns to its natal position after 27+ years, while transiting Saturn takes about 28-29 years to return to its natal position.

These two cycles track each other, and are core indicators of when we confront life-altering choices. Though they are close to the same length, they have different functions in our psychological development, and the difference in timing is significant in how our life unfolds. The progressed Moon symbolizes our inner emotional development, while transiting Saturn demonstrates how maturely and effectively we are handling outer life events.

Because the Moon rules Cancer and Saturn rules Capricorn, and these two signs oppose each other, the Moon and Saturn do a dance as balanced rulers of opposite signs in the same polarity. The Cancer/Capricorn axis represents the primal innocence we're born with, by which we instinctively know the right thing to do without regard for ulterior motives or the need to clutch or manipulate out of insecurity.

℞ Saturn: Spiritual Master, Spiritual Friend

The Moon and Saturn represent opposite ends of the polarity, one emotional and one practical, and work together to craft personality structures which will protect and nurture us and our sense of purpose. As the progressed Moon does its dance with transiting Saturn throughout the years, we find our progressed feelings shaping our choices at critical points, as well as an ever-deeper realization of how the limits in life circumstances are either feeding us or denying us what we need.

THE PROGRESSED LUNAR CYCLE

In Chapter Two we briefly discussed secondary directions, a.k.a. "progressions," and how we calculate them by assuming every day after the birth day is equivalent to one year of time. Thus, our progressed Sun, moving approximately one degree a day, will be about 30 degrees ahead of our natal Sun when we are 30 years old, and will be 45 degrees ahead of the natal Sun position 45 days (progressed years) after birth.

The other planets all progress from their birth positions at varying rates of speed. These variances show us why certain parts of our lives progress at the pace they do. For example, our Mercury and Venus usually progress at a faster rate of speed than our Sun, unless they are near or in their retrograde period. All the other planets progress at slower rates than the Sun except the Moon, which moves faster than any other planet.

The progressed Moon is associated with how we're experiencing life as it proceeds day to day, week to week, and month to month, and symbolizes our evolving feelings in specific progressed areas of our lives. Because the Moon completes its orbit of the Earth every 27.3 days, it indicates around the time we are 27+ years old, we experience a progressed Lunar return. This period has major implications for how we feel about life and our future potential, since it marks the time when, to whatever

191

♄ Saturn: Spiritual Master, Spiritual Friend

degree, we have felt, "up close and personal" all of the sign energies in the zodiac and emotionally experienced an entire cycle of the Moon going through all the signs and houses in our chart.

Since all our planetary points are activated during a complete cycle of the progressed Moon, every part of personality comes under a "feeling scrutiny" with each contact. At the progressed Lunar return we have a type of "completeness" in how we have felt every part of our life and personality. After the first progressed Lunar return, we commence the second transit of the Moon through all the signs and houses between the age of 27 and 54-55, at which point we have the second progressed Lunar return. These 27+ year cycles give us crucial experiential information about how we feel at each step in our Self-unfoldment, since they track how we become aware as all our emotional responses are triggered throughout the "whole cycle" of the progressed Moon.

When the progressed Moon makes important aspects to our planets, it puts a focus on those qualities and triggers emotional responses to memories and activities associated with these planets. Over the span of 27 years, the progressed Moon makes every possible aspect to all our planets, giving us every possible phase relationship between our progressed emotional experience and our natal inclinations. Every conjunction, square, or opposition the progressed Moon makes to a planet or the Ascendant brings phase shifts in how our feelings relate to various parts of our personality. These happen at different times within the 27 years for each of us based in the natal planetary positions.

When the progressed Moon conjuncts our Sun, we get a whole new feel and sensitivity about our natal Light/Life. As it makes all the aspects to the Sun, we are provided points of dynamic change in how we feel about our Light. It is the same with all the other planets. The progressed Moon puts the focus on our innate tendencies each time it conjuncts a natal planet, and how we respond as it makes aspects to that planet gives us information

♄ Saturn: Spiritual Master, Spiritual Friend

about when and how we must nurture the best expression of those personality traits.

A progressed Lunar conjunction always gives us a chance to re-set how we're experiencing and expressing each planetary function. One of the most important contacts is when the progressed Moon conjuncts natal Saturn, because we get an inner emotional reset related to how we feel about our duties, obligations, and perceived deficiencies. Feelings of being weighted down, stifled, or incompetent need to be examined so that we get clear about how to change, leaving behind those things which frustrate us. The progressed Moon conjunct natal Saturn is a crucial point where we get clear about whether our inner Saturn function is expressing our power, or we feel oppressed and very heavy inside. In both cases, we are given unmistakable signals about the health of our inner Saturn.

Throughout life, our progressed Moon makes all the aspects with our natal Saturn, each one revealing how we feel about the burdens of our life, and how willing we are to reject what oppresses us and accept the power to change what we can. Regardless of the aspects made, even the hardest of frictional angles is only as "unfortunate" as we allow it to be. Even if an aspect accompanies difficult or life-shattering events, we still have the power to liberate our view from the limitations of the moment while doing what we must. Then even afflictions become blessings, since they force us to get clear and mobilize on our own behalf.

Along with its profound impact on our personality as it aspects our planets, the progressed Moon also has an equally profound impact on our orientation to the world as it travels through our houses, since each house it moves through brings our focus to the life affairs associated with those sectors. For example, when the progressed Moon conjuncts the Ascendant, we reset our progressed emotional reflection and reaction habits as well as what we care about, what we feel is or isn't necessary, and find new ways to re-shape our self-image which profoundly affects

℞ Saturn: Spiritual Master, Spiritual Friend

the future.

As the Moon moves through the first, second, and third houses, we feel our way to a new identity, and then gather the values, resources, ideas, and view we need to support our emergent feeling-identity. As the progressed Moon moves through the fourth through ninth houses in the chart, we experience what we feel as a result of being in the world of others, moving from a subjective focus in the fourth, fifth, and sixth houses into a more objective focus in the seventh, eighth, and ninth houses. As the progressed Moon moves into the quadrant of the tenth, eleventh, and twelfth houses, we again put the focus on our affairs rather than the world of others, preparing for another major emotional re-set when the progressed Moon again conjuncts our Ascendant.

Since it's related to our inner experience, a progressed Lunar contact may or may not be associated with an obvious real-world event, but they mark points of significant inner decisions related to a way we're living, even if we're not fully aware of the choices we're making, or what they will lead to down the road of life.

In this 27+ year cycle, there are significant quadrant shifts about every seven years depending on how fast or slow the progressed Moon is moving. It is why we seem to confront dramatic changes approximately every seven years. As we discussed in Chapter Seven, these shifts also bear a direct relationship with the transiting squares and oppositions of Saturn to our natal Saturn, as well as other cycles outside the scope of this work.

By examining the progressed Lunar cycle, the transiting Saturn cycle, and noting the decisions and changes taking place at critical points in each of those cycles, we can see larger long wave themes related to the primary nature of our existence. The inner experiential shifts allow us to see our life narratives from a larger perspective over time, and always marks periods of reorienting due to a form of emotional awakening.

These life-altering points are when we naturally

℞ Saturn: Spiritual Master, Spiritual Friend

examine our changing feelings about daily life, our habits, and how we want to live. At the Lunar return we realize we no longer care about some things, and no longer want to express certain personality traits as a result of completing an entire cycle of emotional experience. It is a time when we begin anew, using the visceral emotional wisdom we've acquired over the past 27+ years.

By 27, the progressed Moon has already shown us what we need and don't need, and we're clear about the parts of our lifestyle which no longer nurture our inner Self. This awakened feeling about those things we do and don't care about results from feeling every possible sign expression that led us to a completeness of experience. By the progressed Lunar return, the countless inner changes we've gone through set the emotional foundation for the choices to be made as we approach and enter the Saturn return period following the progressed Lunar return.

SEVEN YEAR SHIFTS - THE PROGRESSED MOON LEADS TRANSITING SATURN

The Moon represents our personal experience of life, whereas Saturn is how we define ourselves and sense of purpose. The latter is how we do it, while the former is how and what we feel while we're doing it. Our natal aspect between these two planetary functions indicates how our feelings relate to our Dharma, and the changes in the relationship between those two parts of ourselves reveal how we are evolving in our experience of life as a function of time.

While all planets have their whole cycle, the dance of the progressed Moon with transiting Saturn indicates how our emotional nature relates to our sense of being limited or fulfilled by the obligations and restrictions related to the larger complex of authorities and structures with their rules and protocols. The progressed Moon represents our internal reaction to things. Transiting Saturn represents

♄ Saturn: Spiritual Master, Spiritual Friend

worldly circumstances where we confront what we will and won't participate in.

Saturn acts as a gatekeeper in each house it transits and reveals what we must learn to have a sense of security in those areas. When it is in the hemisphere of self, we must learn all we need to about our public self and our private self; when it is in the hemisphere in the non-self, we must learn all we need to about functioning in the world of others, both in public and private realms.

As we discussed in Chapter Seven regarding the whole cycle and various "stations" in any cycle, the progressed Moon makes a waxing (lower) square to our natal Lunar position about seven years after birth, more or less depending on the speed of the Moon by progression. This square, occurring when we are young, prepares us for a new experience of day to day life, usually corresponding with beginning elementary school and the realization our parents and the world have rhythms that don't revolve entirely around us.

At this point we begin to adapt instinctively to an active self-expression in the world of others. The forms these will take have been entirely shaped by the family and cultural matrix. Still, this waxing square awakens the feeling one is both similar and different from others in the nuclear unit or "tribe," even if only in an undefined way.

Saturn also makes a waxing (lower) square to its natal position around seven years of age. It is a time when, regardless of our inner emotional changes and crises, we must try to learn as much as we can within the binding circumstances Saturn represents. As an evolving child, it is the first point when we come under the authority of those who are not of our immediate family. We must perform in a world beyond our comprehension, learning its rules and protocols of discipline and order.

The opposition of the progressed Moon to our natal Moon occurs between 12-14 years old, the entry into adolescence. It is a time when many feelings "break the surface" in the realm of others, and we become more sensitive to the Lunar package of personality of others in

♄ Saturn: Spiritual Master, Spiritual Friend

our peer group. This is another radical awakening and reorientation, and leads from that point to a further shaping of our personality in the world of public interactions.

Saturn opposes its natal position around 14, a time when we begin to become oppositional to certain authoritarian patterns we've been living within. It is also when we demonstrate we have mastered (to whatever degree) the rules and expectations we've been under up to then. There is a sense of public visibility, but only as a function of the subjective experience we've lived up to that point. Here we establish a preliminary pattern of being an equal to others in some way, even if many of these patterns will be abandoned as we grow into a greater maturity.

Because Saturn is now firmly in the hemisphere of the "not self," it seems others still have all the power. It is a time when we sense where we "fit in" and where we don't, and confront a dilemma. In some areas, we have to accept certain expectations and conform to roles determined by the elders in our world. However, in other areas where we have realized the social structure is too rigid or oppressive we reject and rebel against certain other-oriented structures through non-conformity, and become oppositional to people, things, and assumptions of who "we should be." This opposition begins a phase of defining ourselves by the ideologies confirming who we believe we are and who we believe we aren't.

At 19-20, the progressed Moon makes a waning, (upper) square to our natal Moon, again marking a shift. This time, the sensitivity relates to our public self, reputation, or feelings about the direction of our life and how others are viewing us as we experience it through our own emotional filters. Then we enter an emotional harvest period, until we get to the Lunar return at 27, where we consolidate parts of our personality in attempts to fulfill our inner needs and those things we care about, whether they are a product of our early matrix or an awakened need for recognition and living life on our own terms.

Saturn makes a waning (upper) square to its natal

Saturn: Spiritual Master, Spiritual Friend

position around 22, marking a culmination of our physical, emotional, and mental structuring. This is a time in life when we feel at ease or oppressed by how we are seen in our society, with all our strengths and vulnerabilities. We begin to see our "power potential" in the world, and claim a form of adulthood on our own terms. It doesn't mean we are free of all the traps and assumptions we grew up with, but it marks a peak in our evolution fulfilling a part of the process in structuring our personality in the public realm.

As with the progressed Moon, this begins a seven year "harvest period" where we capture the harvest of what we have cultivated up to that point, with a greater autonomy to choose who we want to be with, how we want to live, and which ambitions we want to pursue. This phase completes itself as we near the Saturn return between 28-30, when we figure out what parts of our life and relationships no longer work for us. We examine social rules and constructs which no longer apply to us, and begin to move toward our unlived potential, even if we don't know what it is. Then the entire cycle repeats again.

LUNAR RETURNS AND SATURN RETURNS

During the progressed Lunar returns at 27 and 54-55, our feelings go through a fundamental transformation. These periods provide opportunities to take a more objective look at unacknowledged subconscious needs and motivations, and we can examine what we've been resisting or rebelling against. Through accepting the need to replace emotional responses creating strife with those leading to peace, we change compulsive behaviors to more satisfying ways of responding to daily life and its changes

Again, the "reset" to our emotional defaults results from the subconscious mind recognizing we've experienced an entire cycle of all the sign experiences and expressions in the zodiac, and we are somehow more

♄ Saturn: Spiritual Master, Spiritual Friend

complete yet different than we were. We face a new awakened feeling-awareness, and a renewed sense of how we want to experience life in the future, emotionally connected with a sense of the totality of all we've been through up to then. Because of the changes in our emotional nature at the first Lunar return, at the first Saturn return we have enough emotional and worldly experience to know we have the power to choose how we want to make our mark on the world.

At age 27, we are at a peak in our biological cycle. Our hormones are at a peak, our energies are at a peak, and from that point, even if we want to continue, we confront our inability to sustain the previous levels of energy output. Because we just don't care about some things any more, and our needs have changed, this leveling out of physical-biological energy and completion of a whole cycle of feeling-experience leads us to feel the natural limits we must come to grips with in the years after the progressed Lunar return which factor into what we accept at the Saturn return.

After the first progressed Lunar and transiting Saturn returns, we enter a "blue sky" era of pure potential which we pursue in an expanding universe in our 30s, and capture what we can in our 40s before we begin the harvest of our Saturn wisdom in our 50s. This leads us to the second Lunar return in our mid-50s, marking another significant emotional re-set that provides the feeling-foundation for the important changes and decisions at the second Saturn return.

The inner changes associated with the cycle of the progressed Moon either support the subsequent choices associated with transiting Saturn, or lead to an inner sense of a lack or a need. It is the relationship of our inner nature to outer events that conditions our responses to karmic events and therefore our lives. While we come to major endings and beginnings at both the first progressed Lunar return and the first Saturn return, they merely mark the end of the first part of our lives, and lead us directly into the next long term 27-29 period.

₮ Saturn: Spiritual Master, Spiritual Friend

The First Whole Cycle

Progressed Moon and Transiting Saturn

Progressed Moon waning square natal Moon, Age 19 - 20

Transiting Saturn waning square transiting Saturn, Age 22

Natal Moon

Transiting Saturn

Progressed Moon opposes natal Moon, Age 12-14
Transiting Saturn opposes natal Saturn, Age 14

Progressed Moon waxing square natal Moon, Age 7
Transiting Saturn waxing square natal Saturn, Age 7

Subsequent Whole Cycles
Progressed Moon and Transiting Saturn

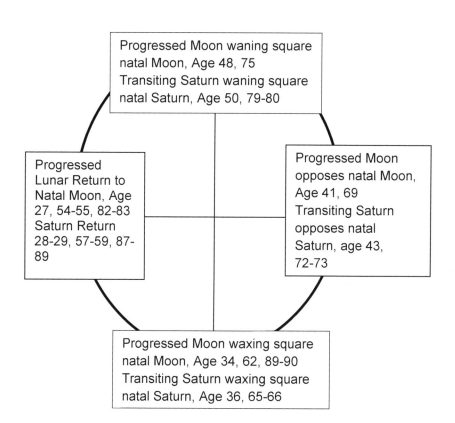

℞ Saturn: Spiritual Master, Spiritual Friend

SUBSEQUENT LIFE SHIFTS

The progressed Moon making its critical shifts just before transiting Saturn indicates that we sense or feel the shift before we confront what we have to do about it. Because of the different lengths of time between the progressed Lunar return and the transiting Saturn return, the gap between the Lunar shifts and Saturn shifts grows in length as we get older.

While the gap between the first progressed Lunar return and the first transiting Saturn return is only about 12-30 months, by the second lunar return at 54-55 we are given a 3 to 4 year gap until we confront the hard realities of the second Saturn return. During this gap, we are offered opportunities to evaluate how we feel about where we're at. By the second Lunar return, we know we've experienced another whole "feeling cycle" and begin to sense that the middle period of life is done. For those fortunate enough to have a third Lunar return and Saturn return in their 80s, the gap between these two events is even greater, with the Lunar return around 82-83 and the Saturn return around 87-89.

So far we've discussed the Lunar and Saturn shifts occurring during the first 29 years of life. We also have Lunar shifts occurring around 34, 41, 48, 54-55, 62, 69, 75-76, 82-83, and 89-90. After the first Saturn return, in the second and third Saturn cycles the shifts occur around 36, 43, 50, 57-59, 65-66, 72-73, 79-80, and 87-89.

Again, these are approximate, since the speed of the Moon and Saturn vary at different times of the year, and even in different signs. And as I explained earlier, because we begin to vibrate to the planetary returns as soon as the planet enters the sign occupied by our natal planets, sometimes we start encountering life-changing experiences well before the exact time of the return.

To bring it all back full circle, if you examine the choices, major decisions, and endings and beginnings accompanying your first progressed Lunar and transiting

♄ Saturn: Spiritual Master, Spiritual Friend

Saturn return, it can make the shifts at the time they form waxing squares to the natal positions around 34-36 a little more comprehensible. Since those course corrections set things into motion defining how we live our purpose in the late 30s and early 40s, it can give us a larger perspective on how the experiences between 27 and 29 led to the feeling changes at 41 and the evolving change in life structures at 43-44.

The repolarization in our early 40s indicated by the progressed Moon opposing the natal Moon and transiting Saturn opposing natal Saturn offers us valuable awarenesses so we may make mid-course adjustments. This is a natural time to make sure we're on track to fulfill the original intention set at the first Saturn return, and maybe even expand it. Around 48 we hit another emotional culmination point affecting our Saturn choices around 49-50.

At 54-55 we move through the second Lunar return and at 57-59 into the second Saturn return, with the major endings and beginnings accompanying those momentous life events. At the second Lunar return we again find we no longer care about certain things, since many potentials have been actualized or are no longer part of our aspirations. On a related note, the decade of our 50s is arguably the most important decade in a human life, due to various progressions and transits occurring then. A study of the astrological events of this decade of life will yield a clear understanding of why we must leave many things behind, creating the space in our life so we may offer the wisdom of our adult experience to the world.

* * * * * * * * *

We are all learning how to transcend patterns keeping us oppressed or off balance. As we mature into spiritual adulthood, we learn over and over that nothing external should be able to distract us from our spiritual equipoise. Even when it does, we can always feel better

♄ Saturn: Spiritual Master, Spiritual Friend

and more empowered as we consciously choose productive responses rather than fall into attachments, aversions, illusions, or pessimism.

All aspects, harmonious and frictional, merely reveal a relationship between the functions of our inner and outer life. While major life changes are sometimes very difficult, they also demonstrate how willing we are to learn, to adapt, to grow, and to see our life purpose from a larger angle of our evolving wisdom on the various levels of human existence. The truth of our eternal Self is to be found in how our perspective has evolved as a result of life experience.

We all are moving from ignorance into mastery. Attitude, willingness, striving, adaptability, perseverance, and a sense of humor in seeking our evolving "Truth of Being" are everything. While often the way to Self-realization is arduous and endlessly involves being mindful as we remove the chains of superstition and erroneous beliefs from our lives, and may even entail the loss of much we've assumed or held precious, I am reminded of a quote from a great Western Spiritual Master that, "Nothing's impossible if you find the right point of view." We are all becoming more than we were, and the possibilities are endless.

♄ Saturn: Spiritual Master, Spiritual Friend

CHAPTER 10

SATURN CONJUNCT PLUTO FOR EVERYONE ON EARTH 2003-2020

This now brings us to the final chapter in our journey, which is of utmost importance to everyone on Earth, as well as those who will be born in the future. So far, we've discussed the many ways Saturn impacts us throughout our lives and in this chapter, we'll explore how and when transiting Saturn conjuncted the Pluto of all generations, and its profound impact on our past, present, and future.

While our inner Saturn is associated with a lot of "shadow material" in our conscious and subconscious minds, there is another planet also associated with our deepest fears, and that's Pluto. Both Saturn and Pluto show us shadow material residing deep within our psyche, with a crucial difference in the types of shadows each planet is related to.

Saturn represents all that binds us as we learn our limitations and live our destiny. It is the furthest boundary of our human-ness. Pluto, "Lord of the Underworld," symbolizes forces of Ultimate Transformation beyond individual control. It is the Limitless Pillar of Infinite Fire associated with Shiva, the eternal process driving the deepest and broadest purification and transformation of all things.

Pluto represents an atomic non-negotiable energy, the pulse of absolute death and rebirth. It is always present in those times and experiences where we confront the

ħ Saturn: Spiritual Master, Spiritual Friend

power of the Firebird to die in its own Divine Fire only to be reborn out of the ashes of what was consumed. It represents the transpersonal transforming power of seeds to eternally replicate their life patterns, bringing forth ever newer forms and forces across vast sweeps of time.

Pluto, because it rules death and rebirth, brings us face to face with our relationship to life and death processes, and its power of relentless purification removes obsolete forms through events which often overwhelm us. Through major upheavals forcing us to understand the transitory nature of all things, Pluto-related events challenge us to sweep away the old husks in our life so we can contact our spiritual core. This is found in our deepest seed-matrix, where the patterns of potential spiritual exist, waiting to be reborn in a life renewal to come at the end of the journey through our personal "underworld."

This part of our existence is related to our journey to personal immortality after all our human dross is stripped away, leaving the purest essence of the Highest Self as an adequate vehicle to express our Soul/Spirit. Because of its very long wave orbit, no one on Earth except the most advanced Yogis have lived an entire Pluto cycle of 250 years. While we all experience many aspects from transiting Pluto to our natal planets, none of us mere mortals ever experience Pluto making all the aspects to all our planets.

PLUTO GUIDES US THROUGH THE UNDERWORLD OF OUR EXISTENCE

Pluto is always present when we find ourselves in those deep and dark places most of us would rather avoid than traverse, because there is an accompanying sense of potential annihilation during Pluto-related experiences. These are events where we must examine every dark corner of our being to make sure we haven't conveniently glossed over those parts of our existence.

♄ Saturn: Spiritual Master, Spiritual Friend

Any time we feel like we are lost in darkness, under pressure and superheated in some way, we are dealing with Pluto. Those are times when we must confront and eliminate whatever is creating shadow material in our self-conscious, subconscious and unconscious minds, becoming more at ease with the eternal and universal process of self-transformation. There's really no way of escape, since the lessons we avoid in this life we'll have to confront at some point in the future, whether this life or the next. No one escapes Karma and Dharma. All things are fulfilled within Karma and Dharma. We all must go through a "dark night of the Soul" to know beyond a shadow of a doubt that If we cannot be at peace in the darkness, we'll never know peace in the Light.

Pluto shows us the way to purify ourselves to our core where we leave behind any possible resistance to our liberation and need for spiritual rebirth. The pressure we feel during those times teaches us perseverance. As we navigate the dark night of the Soul, whether for a few hours or years, we find we will survive and come out stronger and clearer, having eliminated many of the impurities in our personality.

As we learn through experiences associated with "the dark sides of life," we come to see our power to reverse decay, as well as eliminate corrosive elements rotting all they touch. As we claim this power, we find an x-ray vision allowing us to see the most direct route to the core of any matter, where we know what needs to expunged and what needs to be regenerated.

Pluto is unyielding. Through Pluto we find we must live in darkness for as long as it takes for us to accept there are things to be learned in our shadowland. All of us must go through our personal "underworld" at least once in life. The journey changes us forever, and we can find healing and comfort in remembering the part of us that goes down to the underworld is entirely an ego construct. We humans must learn about the underworld of existence so we do not fear it.

℞ Saturn: Spiritual Master, Spiritual Friend

Pluto is associated with life-altering events which compel us to examine elements of our personal "hell," where there is no way out except through our willingness to move into a purifying fire leading to a cleaner, clearer Light of human existence after those experiences. Those who attempt to dodge these unavoidable experiences wind up living in darkness even though the Light is waiting for them after they do the work required to exit their private hell.

Through embracing the Plutonic process, we find at some point even the longest night gives way to the dawning of a new day in our lives. The new Light makes all things clear, bleakness gives way to beauty, and the apprehension of being stuck in unending darkness vanishes, replaced by a measure of joy, hope, and anticipation of things to come. The Light dispels all shadows, and if we have thoroughly examined the underworld of our existence, learning all those things Pluto has to teach us, we never have to go there again.

One added benefit for doing this type of self-purification is over time we become less afraid, whether of what's coming or what's leaving. We all need to find true self-confidence amidst the world's turmoil using the deep and profound truths we find so we can live a more authentic life. Pluto gives us unfettered insights about how to cooperate with the transformative process in a conscious way to find our core spiritual power allowing us to stand fearless in the underworld.

As we become unafraid, then if karma allows us the privilege, we are able to be of service to others going through their dark night of the Soul since we won't fall into fear or uncertainty regardless of their emotional state. When in the underworld, it's nice to have a friend who reminds us we are not alone and there is a way to the Light if only we do the work we need to in our time of darkness. Our friend cannot do the work for us, but they can remind us we're all in this together, and there are universal lessons to be learned, whether in the darkness of worldly existence or the Divine Light of Eternal Existence.

♄ Saturn: Spiritual Master, Spiritual Friend

SATURN SHOWS US THE WAY TO MASTERY AS WE TRANSFORM

Our journey into the underworld is pretty serious business from the angle of the impermanent ego. Even though we must take the trip, and will ultimately be shown our Divine power of eternal self-reinvention, going into the underworld of existence is still terrifying to the ego, bound by Saturn and our Ring Pass Not.

The transformations and hard lessons we go through via Pluto and Saturn are the most harrowing experiences a human can have. The dance of those planets in our lives reveals our spiritual maturity as we move through situations stripping away illusions and obsolete belief systems leaving us transformed. Saturn crystallizes and gives form, focus, and structure to those things Pluto concentrates through its essential nature as Divine Economy of Energy purifying our primary patterns of eternal Self-transformation.

While Pluto is associated with irrevocable loss, Saturn shows us how well we handle those losses and subsequent opportunities for renewal. Our inner Saturn leads us to confront our resistance to change regarding those things seemingly out of our control, and leads us to accept that some things must end so we can expand our understanding and re-focus our destiny and our lives.

Saturn and Pluto together accompany relentless challenges to our sense of freedom and self-transformative regeneration. Because Saturn and Pluto both symbolize ultimate shadow material in primal areas of our consciousness, when they come together in dynamic aspect we confront our deepest fears and accept certain compelling realities as we move through endings and beginnings. As we learn to cooperate with these two planetary energies, we find it easier to be courageous as we move through earth-shaking events, and, demonstrate discipline under pressure.

210

℞ Saturn: Spiritual Master, Spiritual Friend

Pluto is associated with the deaths and radical endings which matter to us, while Saturn helps us understand the necessity of those passages. No matter how difficult the challenges we encounter via Saturn and Pluto, at some point they will pass. All forms pass away, and in practicing detachment, we learn not to clutch at the good, nor get stuck in believing our troubles are here to stay. This helps us stay in the NOW and remember all things in this world are transitory, including our own perceived existence.

The challenges we confront via Saturn and Pluto require cultivating and maintaining a sense of humor to antidote the heavy seriousness accompanying the passage through the underworld of our existence. The ability to see the humor in situations is an invaluable tool as we navigate the fluctuations of life, since laughter sets us free. When we encounter heaviness, we always have the power to laugh at the absurdity of what is, what we imagine, and what will never be. This is the benefit of living in the NOW, and remembering the sage advice to deal with today's problems today, and leave tomorrow's problems for tomorrow.

In the final analysis, we cannot resist the transformations associated with our natal Pluto and the Pluto transits occurring throughout our lives. It would be as impossible as commanding a tsunami to reverse course. However, though the storms swirl around us, with some of the worst throwing us into our worst nightmare, we can come through all of them freed of old psychological baggage.

Our losses can teach us humility and detachment if we find the right point of view, surrendering ego assumptions and rigidities and embracing a greater compassion for the universal human condition. All lessons involving Saturn and Pluto offer us opportunities to transform conditional love into unconditional love, since regardless of what leaves, love endures.

Since all beings go through profound losses at several points in life, our losses and growth into spiritual

♄ Saturn: Spiritual Master, Spiritual Friend

maturity can serve to remind us of what we share with others across space and time, and at key points help us comfort others who also are going through profound loss. This helps us destroy the roots of separateness, and gives us chances to "pay it forward."

Once we get over fear of loss and the unknown, Pluto's transpersonal-transformative power allows us to be our loving, wise, intelligent Self in all dark situations where people are under pressure, or dealing with the underworld of their own existence. Through Pluto, we learn we *are* an immortal, Divine spark of Light within a field of Limitless Light, and there is nothing preventing us from questing, realizing, and applying our skills as we become the Master of our reality.

TRANSITING SATURN CONJUNCT NATAL PLUTO
THE LARGER CYCLIC SWEEP

Transiting Saturn conjunct our Pluto brings a definite conclusion to some seed patterns which cannot grow into the future, while introducing Plutonic structures which will yield favorable transformational growth in the years after this transit. This combination brings radical long term pressures and changes, often with explosive force, overwhelming obsolete assumptions and personality weaknesses.

Since Saturn structures or restructures whatever it touches, when it comes to visit Pluto, our lives are restructured and purified from top to bottom. Because natal Pluto is a non-dual Divine Power, which is the vehicle for ultimate Self-realization and Self-transformation, Saturn conjunct Pluto crystallizes that power, usually associated with events triggering our deepest fears arising from the most profound endings and beginnings any of us will ever have. When transiting Saturn (external situations testing our ability to restructure toward perfection away from unnecessarily limiting conditions) conjuncts our natal

212

♄ Saturn: Spiritual Master, Spiritual Friend

Divine Transpersonal Transformative seed power, we are offered blessings liberating us forever.

Saturn will usually conjunct your Pluto at least once, and often twice in your lifetime. If you live long enough, some people in rare circumstances even experience it three times. Each time brings us life-altering changes affecting the core of our existence. While those periods can crystallize our worst apprehensions and lower qualities, they also assist us in confronting our Divine Power of transforming the lower self into the Higher Self.

As we respond to events related to Saturn-Pluto contacts, we fulfill and restructure long range karma which leads us into long range disciplines so various seeds of our Higher Self can come forth as Dharma dictates. Saturn conjunct the natal Pluto establishes a new Ring-Pass-Not boundary within which some form of crystallized Divine Power will be established for the next whole Saturn cycle.

Since the transit of Saturn to a natal Pluto takes a year or more, it brings lessons to learn on first conjunction, a new look at the same lessons while retrograde but from different angles of approach, and at the third passage we implement what we've learned up to then. While those transits can be difficult, they are not necessarily impossible to deal with, and the difficulties we encounter are exactly what we need to grow.

These periods are watersheds of personal evolution, since they are associated with how willing we are to end lesser ways of living, moving through the transformational process so we can express our spiritual power. When Saturn conjuncts Pluto, we experience deep and profound changes dividing the waters of past and future forever.

213

♄ Saturn: Spiritual Master, Spiritual Friend

WHEN THE LORD OF FEAR MEETS THE LORD OF THE UNDERWORLD, EITHER YOU KILL YOUR FEAR OR IT KILLS YOU

Saturn represents the issues we may have related to controlling or manipulating others, or being controlled or manipulated by a thing, person, or idea. When it comes to visit the "Lord of the Underworld," we find the means to break free of our deepest fears, or be consumed by them.

Saturn limits and binds all it touches; the Lord of the Underworld cannot be limited or bound. These contacts are times to surrender, in humility, to the reality showing us we have met those things we fear the most, and we'll either succumb to fear or master it. Here it's useful to remember we are not alone as we go through our ordeals, since we share a Pluto position with tens of millions of others who are alive because we were all born during that generation.

The natal Pluto position indicates generational power, as well as what each generation needs to purify at the core of their being. Pluto is where we find our power to transform our lives radically and completely in an ever-renewing spiritual Electric Fire. When transiting Saturn conjuncts our natal Pluto, we are offered the opportunity to structure that power so it serves us in perfectly expressing our Divine Self.

During the times transiting Saturn makes conjunctions with the Pluto of various generations, everyone affected must take an honest look at their relationship to the "underworld" of their existence and bring forth a mature spiritual power while expunging corrosive elements from their life. This brings extreme energies and extreme situations into play, and demonstrates how well we're dealing with ours or others' shadow material.

Because of the varying lengths of time Pluto spends in different signs, some Pluto generations get more Saturn conjunctions than others, and some clusters of generations are impacted in a shorter time than others.

214

♄ Saturn: Spiritual Master, Spiritual Friend

Saturn conjunct the Pluto of a cluster of generations represents an evolutionary challenge unlike any known in a lifetime, because over a relatively short period of time, everyone on Earth has to confront restructuring their lives in radical ways.

At this time on Earth, everyone who is alive (with very few exceptions) has been born since 1914 when Pluto was in Cancer. Since the Summer of 2003, Saturn has conjuncted the Pluto of every generation born since 1914. This means everyone on Earth has dealt with some form of very heavy transformation, or has been put under relentless pressure to restructure and purify their Plutonic energy.

PLUTO – PAST AND PRESENT

In this section we'll examine the signs Pluto has occupied since it began this "turn of the cosmic wheel" when it entered Aries in the early 19th century. During the decades Pluto was in Apehelion, or the slowest speed in its orbital path around the Sun, it took almost a century to transit Aries, Taurus, and Gemini. This period lasted from 1822 through 1914, and was marked by one of the most important celestial events in terms of long wave human evolution, the Neptune-Pluto conjunction in Gemini occurring off and on between 1888 and 1897. This marked the end of a quarter of a Great Age, since the previous Neptune conjunct Pluto occurred at the end of the 14th and beginning of the 15th century, also in early Gemini.

During the time Pluto was in Aries, Taurus, and Gemini, for about seven years out of every 29 everyone on Earth experienced Saturn on their Pluto. Even with the shorter life spans, some 19th century beings experienced Saturn on their Pluto as many as three times in their lives.

However, since Pluto's speed quickened for most of the 20th century, it transited more signs than it had the previous century. From 1914-2000, it moved through

♄ Saturn: Spiritual Master, Spiritual Friend

Cancer, Leo, Virgo, Libra, Scorpio, and early Sagittarius. At this time in history it takes Saturn about 14 years out of every 29 to touch the Pluto of everyone on Earth, offering a wider and therefore richer experience since it traverses a larger spread of zodiac energies.

When Saturn entered Cancer in the Summer of 2003, it began a long period of conjunctions to the Pluto positions of everyone alive on Earth. As Saturn transited through subsequent signs between 2005 and now (2016), it has formed conjunctions with the Pluto in Leo, Virgo, Libra, Scorpio, and Sagittarius generations. This has impacted every person on Earth. All of us have experienced Saturn's influence on the deepest part of our Being. Children born with Pluto in Sagittarius and Capricorn have had or will have experienced Saturn conjunct their Pluto for the first time between 2015 and 2020.

This will not happen again until the era which begins in 2034, when Saturn returns to the Pluto in Leo generation. That mass restructuring will last until 2054, since Saturn will have completed Pluto conjunctions for those who are alive with Pluto in Leo, Virgo, Libra, Scorpio, Sagittarius, and Capricorn.

Saturn's transit of Aquarius and the first half of Pisces between 2050 and 2054 will be the first Saturn conjunct Pluto for those with Pluto in Aquarius and the first half of Pisces. Those born with Pluto in Aries or Taurus (2067-2118) will have to wait until 2114 through 2118 for their first transit of Saturn over their Pluto. To bring it full circle, Pluto was last in Gemini between 1882 and 1914, so the last time that generation experienced Saturn conjunct their Pluto was 2001-2003, and before then, 1971-74. Almost all of this generation has passed from the Earth at this time.

♄ Saturn: Spiritual Master, Spiritual Friend

SATURN CONJUNCT THE PLUTO IN CANCER, LEO, AND VIRGO GENERATIONS

In the next two sections, we'll explore the Plutonic time spans of all generations on Earth. You will note that there are generational overlaps, where Pluto entered the next sign, and then retrograded back into the previous sign. These positions are a generational bridging influence, marking the end of an old generation and the beginning of a new one.

Pluto in Cancer

The Pluto in Cancer generation, those born between September 1912 and June 1939 (with a few exceptions at the front end who have Pluto in Gemini), went through three major restructuring periods when Saturn transited Cancer. The first was from the Summer of 1944 through the summer of 1946. The second was from the Summer of 1973 through the Summer of 1976, and the most recent one was between the Summer of 2003 through Summer 2005. These periods were times of major endings and beginnings for the War Generation.

All people born during the first four decades of the 20th century who were still alive began their part of the global restructuring between 2003-2005 (the 1900-1912 group had Saturn conjunct their Neptune in Cancer and Pluto opposing their Pluto in Gemini!) Because the 1912-1939 group was born with Pluto in Cancer, it primarily affected their home, family life, their ability to secure their basic needs, and gave them a new feeling-structure to embrace the Divine Transformative energies of Pluto. Most of them will not be around the next time Saturn is in Cancer beginning the Summer of 2032.

217

♄ Saturn: Spiritual Master, Spiritual Friend

Pluto in Leo

The Pluto in Leo generation was born between August 1938 and June 1958. This group is the front end of the "Baby Boom" generation, and constitutes the vast majority of people alive at the time this book is being written. The Pluto in Leo generation have also been through two or three major restructurings due to Saturn transits of Leo, depending on the year they were born.

The first was between the Summer of 1946 and the Spring of 1949. That affected all those born between the August 1938 and Summer of 1947. Those born after the Saturn-Pluto conjunction of 1947 have their first transit of Saturn conjunct Pluto when Saturn was in Leo between Autumn 1975 and Summer 1978, with all groups affected during the most recent one between Summer 2005 and Summer 2007. Those with Pluto in Leo who live to an advanced age will experience it again between August 2034 and July 2037 when Saturn again transits Leo.

As Leo is the sign of the Fixed Fire of the Heart, and Pluto is said to be "exalted" in Leo, this generation has the power of heart, love, creativity, and joy of natural self-expression. Used wisely, this position expresses the power of Divine Transformation using purified heart energy creatively and precisely.

During the period Saturn transited their Pluto in Leo, it brought forth confrontations of mortality, and offered chances to become more spiritually mature, utilizing Divine power to transform their consciousness and their view of power. During these periods, this generation was challenged to eliminate any heart rigidity or hesitancy around expressing their natural loving self and, over time, reshape their Divine Power of the exalted Pluto in Leo to express it more effectively. Some of this group literally became "the authority of the Divine transformational power of the heart" through Saturnine disciplines applied to purification, economy of energy, seed form focus, and everything else Pluto is associated with.

218

♄ Saturn: Spiritual Master, Spiritual Friend

Pluto in Virgo

The Pluto in Virgo generation was born between October 1956 and July 1972. This group has been through their radical restructuring only twice this lifetime. The first time was November and December 1977, and August 1978 through September 1980. The most recent time was from September 2007 through October 2009 and again April through July 2010.

As Virgo is the sign of Divine Discrimination and practical training for some kind of service, this group has the power to purify, transform, or sprout the seeds of the future through bringing forth pioneering new forms in the health and service fields. They are here to repair whatever needs it using their power to make necessary practical adjustments to circumstances.

The choices, decisions, purpose and wisdom this generation distilled out of their experience of mid-2007 through mid-2010 set important patterns into motion directly affecting what they will go through about 20 years from now. The Pluto in Virgo generation will still be alive the next time Saturn goes through Virgo between October 2036 and November 2039, which will again completely transform all of them at the core of their Being.

SATURN CONJUNCT THE PLUTO IN LIBRA, SCORPIO, SAGITTARIUS, AND CAPRICORN GENERATIONS

Pluto in Libra

The Pluto in Libra generation was born between October 1971 and October 1983 (except mid-April through late July 1972), with a few more in the Summer of 1984. This group has had Saturn conjunct their Pluto twice since they were born, and for some, only once. Saturn transited Libra between September 1980 and November 1982, and

219

ħ Saturn: Spiritual Master, Spiritual Friend

most recently between late October 2009 and April 2010, as well as July 2010 through October 2012. The next time this generation will have Saturn transit their Pluto will be between 2039 and 2042.

Pluto in Libra was a time when ideals of relationship went through a complete transformation on a global social level, and by the mid-1980s, we had the seeds of a new sense of equality, proportionality, and justice in the public arena. During that period people backed off of the general intensity of the 1960s, and embraced a different way of relating to each other.

When Saturn transits its exaltation sign of Libra, we are offered possibilities to mature and become more responsible through authoring various forms of "Right Relationship." During the time it conjuncted the Divine Transformer and purifier in Libra, new standards involving principles and ideals of justice, fairness, balance, perspective, and law were introduced. This generation had to confront their rules and assumptions about relationships and over time reshape their responses to better express the Divine power of Libra. Some of this generation became "the authority of the Divine transformational power of relationship" if they made friends with Saturn before or during this period.

Pluto in Scorpio

Those born between November 1983 and November 1995 have Pluto in Scorpio. While most of this generation has experienced only one transit of Saturn on their Pluto, some have had two. Though Saturn was in Scorpio between December 1982 and May 1983, the first time any of this generation experienced Saturn conjunct Pluto was after it returned to Scorpio in August 1983 and transited their Pluto between November 1983 and November 1985. That means the earliest in this group experienced Saturn conjunct Pluto when they were infants and toddlers. More recently, Saturn transited Scorpio

220

℞ Saturn: Spiritual Master, Spiritual Friend

between October 2012 and December 2014, with an encore between mid-June and mid-September 2015.

Pluto in Scorpio is a position of relentless intensity, deep wisdom, and the power of absolute regeneration as it casts out all things which cannot be taken into the unknown future. While capable of living in great darkness, it also represents the depth-purification required of all who would know absolute transcendence. Pluto in Scorpio thrives on power, as well as the dance of intense magnetism with what they want, what they are able to attract, and what they feel they need to repel.

The lessons of structure, responsibility, duty, and self-discipline Saturn brought to this group between October 2012 and September 2015 (except for mid-June through mid-September 2015) began the long wave transformational process for this generation. Late 2012 through late Summer 2015 sprouted seeds of wisdom which will develop through late 2041, helping this generation to be more effective in participating in the larger global evolutionary process. This will bear fruit between November 2041 and September 2043.

Pluto in Sagittarius

Those born between January and April 1995, November 1995 and January 2008, and June through November 2008 have Pluto in Sagittarius. This generation is experiencing their first transit of Saturn on their Pluto. Saturn entered Sagittarius in late December 2014 and stayed there until June 2015. It re-entered Sagittarius in September 2015, and stays in Sagittarius until December 2017.

Pluto in Sagittarius is a position that sees limitless seeds of potential futures, core truths, and concepts of universal law, while casting out obsolete philosophies, religious systems, and narrow views. This generation knows the seeds of eternal truth behind all transformational

221

ℏ Saturn: Spiritual Master, Spiritual Friend

processes, and will sprout seeds of higher awareness bearing fruit for centuries to come.

While this position can produce extremists and ideologies going everywhere and nowhere, it is also good for understanding the absolute freedom we have as Eternals to explore what we need to of the human experience, freed from social restrictions. Pluto in Sagittarius finds power in freedom, discovery, questing, and seeing life as a grand series of experiments in truth.

Pluto in Sagittarius killed the seeds of some futures, while setting other seeds into motion which will create new openings over time. This was a period when humanity experienced "the Grand Irrationality" during the years Neptune made a septile (a powerful 7th harmonic aspect) to Pluto, something we hadn't experienced since the 1930s. During the years Pluto was in Sagittarius, all of humanity moved through a series of radical turning points involving crucial choices and changes affecting the collective destiny of the nations and individuals for centuries to come.

The next time this generation will experience Saturn conjunct their Pluto will be February-March 2044, November 2044 through January 2047, and July through October 2047. Many things set into motion between late 2014 and late 2017 will bear fruit then. This generation will experience another transit of Saturn on their Pluto from December 2073 through December 2076.

Pluto in Capricorn

Those born between January and June 2008, late November 2008 through March 2023, and June 2023 through January 2024 have Pluto in Capricorn. This generation experiences their first transit of Saturn on their Pluto between late December 2017 and March 2020, and a final time July through December 2020.

This will be a crucial conjunction, because transiting Saturn will conjunct transiting Pluto in Capricorn

♄ Saturn: Spiritual Master, Spiritual Friend

in January 2020. Then it moves into a part of the sign which Pluto will not transit until 2021-2023. So it will be the first Saturn conjunct Pluto for those born before 2020, while those born 2020 and after will not experience Saturn conjunct their Pluto until the next transit of Saturn in Capricorn between January and July 2047 and October 2047 through January 2050. After 2050 Saturn will not return to Capricorn until 2076-2079.

Pluto in Capricorn is a time of power struggles on a global level, and clashes between economic and political philosophies. This symbolizes heavy handed authority models, coercion, manipulation, and absolutism in the political sphere, as well as deeply corrosive forces at play in positions of power. In this era, governments go bad, corruption is exposed for all to see, with a need for radical purification in how societies are structured.

Pluto in this sign is killing out old seeds of social protocols and respect for pre-existing systems, purging some governments of any sense of social responsibility, with strong forces of demagoguery holding the world stage. This era will bring about wide spread transformation in how various elements of the world economy and trade are structured, and we're seeing the appearance of extreme ideologies desiring power at all costs. It is an era of authoritarians, as well as the seeds of a more mature sense of responsibility in leaders across the world.

As with the Pluto in Sagittarius generation, this one also is associated with "the Grand Irrationality" of Neptune septile Pluto. Neptune's various sign positions as it made septiles to Pluto in Sagittarius and Capricorn between the mid-1990s and 2017 set humanity's long term global destiny into motion via the sign energies in the "harvest third" of the zodiac, those being Sagittarius through Pisces. This period is one which put seeds into motion yielding major changes for centuries to come.

Saturn, ruling Capricorn, is at home in that sign, and a very dominant force in the world. Saturn finds itself resting easy with its natural expression in Capricorn, and "rules the roost" in that sector of the zodiac. Saturn's transit

223

♄ Saturn: Spiritual Master, Spiritual Friend

through Capricorn will bring a restructuring of how Pluto operates in Capricorn, and brings an old Saturn-Pluto cycle to a close while opening another one.

* * * * * * * * *

As you can see, we have been and continue to be in the heart of a span of 17 years that are crucial in the process of both individual and collective transformation as we approach the threshold of the Age of Aquarius. We have all had opportunities to mature and restructure how the seed-power of our Divine Self sprouts in the world by utilizing the Divine Power of Economy of Energy to purify our life functions.

If you're in a group experiencing Saturn on your Pluto now or in the future, use Saturn's best qualities to become a world-changer in your unique way and place. Saturn transits over Pluto restructures our Ring-Pass-Not, allowing us to claim the power to sprout spiritual seeds that will bear fruit in decades to come. As we bring forth the best possible manifestation of this contact, we will know fear has no power to hinder us. As we learn how to skillfully utilize these powerful inner functions, we will change our lives and world for the better, and become spiritual adults embodying eternal Love, Wisdom, and Intelligence now and across time.

♄ Saturn: Spiritual Master, Spiritual Friend

EPILOGUE
LIVING THE SPIRITUAL LIFE

We now come to the end of this particular journey, prepared for greater adventures to come, with Saturn as our Friend and Guide. As we move into the future, we can access Saturn's self-renewing dedication to the Aquarian ideal we have claimed as our own, as well as the Capricornian persistence of following through, doing what must be done, so that each step is attained in the perfect way and time.

As we walk on in our search for the meaning and purpose of our life, regardless of which paths we follow, we always find new ways to understand that our eternal Self is at one with the stars. We discover countless ways our birth stars reveal facets of our Divine expression as we move through the constantly evolving celestial patterns we all live within. We do a dance throughout eternity as one "energy life" together, and since movement is never ending in the Cosmic Manvantara ("Day of Creation"), to live is to vibrate on many levels, resonating to countless energy fields in our existence.

The unique Divine pattern we were born under perfectly illustrates our path to Self-realization through the material, emotional, mental, and spiritual lessons we learn so our Divine Self can be made manifest this lifetime. By understanding the promise of our Highest Self as revealed in the birth chart, we realize we have the power to embody our unique purpose and catch glimpses of ever-more perfect forms of self-expression. Our stars are the vehicles through which we look without, go within, and find Love

♄ Saturn: Spiritual Master, Spiritual Friend

and Wisdom along the way as we explore all we are to learn across the twelve "frequency zones" of human experience.

The Divine Life is always presenting itself for our consideration and participation, and we all find the way right for us in each unfolding season of our lives. As we become spiritually mature, countless ways open for us to ground a living expression of Love and Wisdom within the Divine Pattern of the time and place we are in. At each level of self-mastery, our planets will increasingly express the qualities of our Divine Self. As we shape and re-shape our learned physical-material, emotional-social, and mental-spiritual constructs, we find we are never limited by the stars or any external factor when given the opportunity to demonstrate the highest spiritual qualities we are able. Because our true nature is eternal, infinite, and unconditional Love, we merely rediscover ever-newer abilities to express it within the pattern of the moment.

As we evolve and become more aware and expert at dealing with life challenges, it is natural to want to achieve as much as possible as quickly as possible. While we can change almost any pattern in the here and now, it takes a bit of practice before we make that new pattern an ingrained habit. Also, timing is everything, since we cannot solve tomorrow's problems today, nor can we move beyond the inherent limits of the immediate moment.

There are natural limits to what we are able to understand and utilize skillfully during any given period in our personal, interpersonal, and transpersonal evolution. This is where, as we master different ways to break free of assumptions that stifle our imagination, we come to understanding and wisdom about form and process.

Throughout life, we learn through time and change that every ending is followed by a new beginning, and when a chapter ends, our ever-renewing Eternal Self again chooses its future course of evolution as a Spirit in the material world, learning to express feelings and thoughts of a higher nature. Our future is limited only by how fit we are to achieve the goals we are trying to accomplish. Some

♄ Saturn: Spiritual Master, Spiritual Friend

who would be ineffective in one realm would be considered geniuses in another medium. That's why our wisdom is cultivated by what we embrace and reject, finding a deeper understanding of our path of infinite growth.

One valuable tool helping us make wise choices involves cultivating the ability to "think in the future." Thinking in the future enables us to anticipate possibilities so we may act in the present and be well-positioned in the future. If we neither overestimate nor underestimate our ability to be effective as those future conditions occur, we will find that each one brings opportunities to practice our evolved skills. Many things are possible if we drop excess baggage and ignore irrelevant considerations as we anticipate and position ourselves for the future. Through practice, we learn to be skilled in managing actions, feelings, and thoughts so we are exactly as we need to be while the future unfolds.

As Eternals having human experiences, each step into the future offers us a practicum in demonstrating personal forms of material, emotional, mental, and spiritual mastery, as well as opportunities to apply our realizations effectively across the interpersonal and transpersonal dimensions of human existence. All our personal skills must be translated into interpersonal skills and the ability to navigate transpersonal realms of life. Our Ring-Pass-Not clarifies each field of activity, and expands as we overcome fear in all realms, allowing us a constant possibility of approaching the threshold of Revelation.

The Ring-Pass-Not is always under pressure by transpersonal forces pushing our boundaries beyond old limitations. Each time we are pushed to the limit of our abilities or understanding, we feel a quickening due to the increased tension of breaking through old limits. Each step we take into the unknown changes the limits of our Ring-Pass-Not, and creates a tension between the edge of our process and the forces that beckon us to become an exemplar, or avatar, in our field of existence and realm of spiritually responsible activity. As we master each stage leading to more perfect expressions of the Higher Self, we

℞ Saturn: Spiritual Master, Spiritual Friend

find we can lift the bar from the Gates of Gold and claim our Divine estate. At some point, we find we have become the teacher we seek, since there is no true separation between the Teacher, the Teaching, and we who are Taught.

SPIRITUAL KARMA AND MAGNETICS

We are all born with a special spiritual karma to fulfill. We move into a greater spiritual effectiveness when we learn to focus on the greatest good for the greatest number, since as we generate positive responses, overcoming the deficiencies and inertias in the field, we send magnetic energy that can be used by all those who are receptive to that positivity. When everyone is benefited then we are as well.

We all have the capacity to cultivate compassion, and this affords us a certain protection as we move through life's storms. Because our essential nature is Love, we are altruistic and idealistic beings. Because we have a somewhat undisciplined lower triad of personality, we learn unfortunate habits that divert our higher energies to lesser behaviors.

We all have excellent talents, but often suffer from a lack of largeness of vision. If we could live in the Eternal Now witnessing our Divine "Is-Be-ness" we would not fall into traps of feeling inadequate arising from ego limitations. That's why from time to time we need to monitor learned internal rules and expectations so previous experiences don't taint our expectations of the good we could achieve in the moment.

Expectations create results due to our power to magnetize life experiences and create patterns which will have an effect in the future. If we can learn to expect positive results even in the midst of difficulty, we can change the magnetics and bring forth the best attainable results. Our striving is assisted by cultivating deep

ħ Saturn: Spiritual Master, Spiritual Friend

meditations, since they allow the personality to align with the Higher Self and attract what is true, good, and beautiful with specificity.

All life's difficulties are impermanent and how we experience them can be changed by how we perceive them. Once we clear our ego-mind of undermining attitudes and work with the world of form using time as our ally, if something is true for us, it will be made manifest at some point. When we stop giving power to negative states, we learn how to transmute and reverse those patterns which result in suffering, since we begin to operate on a level beyond these negative attractors. Here it's useful to frame every challenge, every difficulty, as giving us the power to choose a loving response rather than a not-loving response.

Even in the midst of unfortunate circumstances, we can generate beneficial and altruistic thoughts, words, feelings, and deeds if we want to. We can always find the way to a greater good when we open our imagination and claim the power to create positive and effective thought forms, one step at a time, in our unending journey into the future. As we become more skilled in this, we stop attracting future problems, and create beneficial karmas by virtue of our heart's ability to attract its perfect delight. We have far more power to bring forth positive manifestations than we believe. We only need to shift our point of view and do what it takes to identify consciously with our Divine Essence, and be patient as the magic of Spirit works unerringly to bring forth what is in the Divine plan, which is always a greater good.

As we embrace Divine protection and Grace, welcoming creative challenges to grow spiritually and achieve a greater worldly effectiveness, everything changes forever. Even when we go through losses and apparent defeats, it gives us opportunities to eliminate negative thoughts and feelings, decreasing their power to create negative conditions in the future. The miracle of the evolutionary process is even when we seem to have drifted into a path that is contrary to our best interests, we can still

♄ Saturn: Spiritual Master, Spiritual Friend

wind up in circumstances perfect for our wisdom to come forth.

As we cooperate with the process of coming out of ignorance into awareness, we find the heart is the crystal through which we directly experience all true enlightened states of Being. The heart is a muscle which becomes stronger with exercise, and our hearts are often tested so we may become stronger in our loving radiance. When we have the courage to face everything that life throws at us with compassion and a willingness to grow, over time we find fewer things, events, or people hindering our embrace of the dance with the Eternal, and can generate an intense positivity that cuts through the sources of suffering like a laser beam.

THE SEVEN ENERGIES OF EXISTENCE

In learning to navigate infinite experience, we must master seven universal energies. All of us deal with these seven Rays, or Divine energies, which pervade every part of our existence. Several of them are active in how we express our personalities, the groups and people and ideas we have an affinity for, and even our national, racial, and cultural identification. While a thorough examination of them would require many thousands of pages, to sum them up here, they are:

1st Ray – Will/Power
2nd Ray - Love/Wisdom
3rd Ray - Intelligence in Action
4th Ray - Harmony through Friction/Art
5th Ray - Concrete Knowledge/Science
6th Ray – Devotion/Idealism
7th Ray - Ordered Activity

These are impersonal energies which are expressed in infinite ways. They permeate every aspect of

231

♄ Saturn: Spiritual Master, Spiritual Friend

our existence, and as we realize, apply, and learn to utilize each and all of these with skill, individually and in various combinations, we find a wider understanding about how they manifest in our lives, the lives of others, and the events of the times in which we live.

They are present in the essential nature of all things, including planes of consciousness, individual chakras (energy fields in the body), centers of power in a city, state, or nation, within individual groups and between groups aligned to similar causes, the Earth as a whole, and even the Solar System. On every level, the expression of each and all of these is grounded in a host of Beings who act as vehicles for these energies to manifest in the world.

USING THE RAYS TO ACHIEVE MASTERY OVER THE PROCESS

We learn about these seven energies throughout life in a multitude of ways. They provide the means for us to master those things we're here to cultivate, and show us the stages in everything we would become skilled at. The process of mastering anything involves using the Ray energies in reverse order to bring us from a lack of structure to the highest refined expression of Divine qualities. Since all endeavors require some form of structural order, all disciplines begin with the energies of the Seventh Ray.

The initial stage of mastering anything begins by accepting the need to learn the order and structure of the field we are attempting to learn. The entry into a discipline often entails "doing it by rote." This is where we learn the basic building blocks of any field of endeavor, and have to figure out what fits where within that larger area of potential mastery. These all involve working with Seventh Ray energy.

After learning the basic knowledge, principles, and ordered action in a field, we move into a phase where we

Saturn: Spiritual Master, Spiritual Friend

are practicing what we need to do and have embraced the learning process in an active way, but still don't have much understanding of the activity, field, or effort. This period involves being devoted to doing the practice without enough knowledge to know if we're doing it in a way which is right for us. Often this stage is marked by feelings of incompetence and some confusion. This phase of being devoted to the process involves the Sixth Ray energies.

This period lasts until we finally have enough knowledge related to our striving so we actually "know" the subject matter or practice to whatever degree we have achieved. We then are at the "concrete knowledge" stage of the quest, and are learning many facts and finding the widest breadth of information. Obviously, this is the Fifth Ray stage in the developing process. Still, even though we may acquire extensive knowledge of a field, it doesn't mean we have reached the next stage of finding the "art" of our field of inquiry or practice.

That phase of finding ways to express the art of what we have learned involves utilizing many forms of knowledge and finding "harmony through friction" by blending and shaping the knowledge of the field into a unique, balanced way of articulating one's special approach to the skills being mastered. It is a developmental stage of transcending the different and often conflicted or contradictory approaches to something and using Fourth Ray energy to find the "art" of synthesizing knowledge in specialized ways.

Think back on when you first started your profession or an avocation. You had to learn the functional nuts and bolts of what to do and how to do it. There was no expertise at that stage, and a lot of insecurity while trying to figure out how to bring order out of the chaos of what you still did not know. As you learned the basics of what to do and how to do it, you became aware that you naturally understood some of it, but didn't understand other elements of your area of interest, and had to be devoted to doing the best you could, despite your relative lack of knowledge and experience.

℞ Saturn: Spiritual Master, Spiritual Friend

At some point you became familiar with enough of your craft to be able to "know" many different elements of it, and had more than one approach to understand and deal with all that came up. You had concrete knowledge of the field, but you knew you had to keep learning other approaches and other angles of understanding to come to an ever-greater overview of all there was to know about your area of emerging expertise. As you can see, this can also be applied to any area of personal interest.

Those who pursue a well-rounded approach to knowing their craft ultimately find they have found their unique way of expressing what they know and demonstrating their expertise in their craft. This is the stage where we move from "knowing" a lot to being able to express that knowledge in our own special way. That is the art of the craft.

This applies to our spiritual evolution as well. We begin with learning the basics of a practice we believe is a pathway to a form of "higher awareness." Naturally, we usually do not experience any sort of higher awareness when trying to bring some sense of order out of the chaos of the scattered knowledge and approaches we're just learning. As we learn the basic precepts and practices of a spiritual discipline, we then find we must be devoted to our study and practice even if we don't feel confident or that we're "doing it the right way." We must persist despite inner and outer voices of doubt that arise because our knowledge and experience still feel inadequate as we compare the ideal we imagine with our mind's judgments about what we do not know.

Over time we find we have acquired an ever-greater knowledge of that spiritual practice, can discuss the precepts and practices with some confidence, and may have found a few approaches that led us to forms of intermittent higher awareness. This is also the stage of the "six blind men trying to describe an elephant," since we still are working off of knowledge rather than a holistic awareness arising from direct experience beyond knowledge.

♄ Saturn: Spiritual Master, Spiritual Friend

As we allow the mind to synthesize various things we believe we know, our unique way of experiencing and expressing the higher Truths of our Path comes forth. That is the art of our enlightenment, and allows us to contribute to the rich textures of our Path using the spiritual understanding we have. In finding the art of our spirituality, we often see the truths we've discovered have elements in common with other paths to higher awareness. The more holistic our view, the easier it is to open to core universal truths we share with others.

These stages of development represented by the Rays are at work in each of the three great "Schools of Enlightenment" in the greater evolutionary system. Whether in Art, Science, or Philosophy, if we would master any part of these Schools, we must have an initial ordered approach, followed by a period of being devoted to pursuing the practice of the basics and acquiring further knowledge. When enough knowledge of the art, science, or philosophy has been achieved, then we are able to find our unique approach and synthesize the knowledge we have into unique ways of expressing what we know. As we keep shaping and re-shaping the knowledge we have and how we articulate it, eventually we find our uniquely artistic way of offering what we know to our world.

All of the initial four stages of effort, regardless of the field in which they must be applied, lead us to understanding how the power of the first three Rays infuses all activity leading to any form of relative perfection or enlightenment in any endeavor. The first three Rays represent the power, magnetism, love, wisdom, and intelligence of Spirit pervading any and all efforts in the fields we are mastering.

The first, second, and third Rays also demonstrate as the triad of Higher Laws at work in the Earth's system, those being Economy of Energy, Magnetic Attraction, and Synthesis. It is why all truly great artists, scientists, and philosophers of every stripe have these qualities evident in their lives and specialized expressions of their craft.

Regardless of the general and specific path to

235

♄ Saturn: Spiritual Master, Spiritual Friend

enlightenment we're on, the seven Rays show us the seven Divine energies we're learning to utilize in this seven-fold reality. Even when we acquire a degree of adeptship along certain Ray lines, we continue to be called to learn ever greater skills in more than one musical key of life. A musician uses all the tones at their disposal. We learn to use all the Ray energies as we create the art of our Life.

THE WAY BEYOND EGO

There is a Way beyond our lower ego and its limitations, but to get beyond the lower ego, we first must develop it as a worthy vehicle to express the Higher Ego, or Higher Self. Lower ego must be fully developed if we are to transcend it. Our inner Saturn allows us to scrutinize and examine our ego-mind and its assumptions as we explore why we believe we want what we want, and why we have a sense of who we are that makes us distinct from others we know. Ego wants to control all it encounters, and compartmentalizes everything into convenient categories. Ego likes more, better, and different, as long as it all fits into its comfortable assumptions.

As ego-mind keeps finding more and more information, it begins to realize there are many things it has never conceived of, and turns its focus to bring all those realizations together so they work to bring into manifestation what the ego-mind desires. However, in attempting to bring together everything it thinks it knows, ego-mind eventually confronts the fact that it cannot fit all it perceives into a convenient view it can control. This brings our ego-mind to a crisis. It knows what it knows, but also knows it has received information that does not fit into its preconceptions.

At that point, ego-mind must choose; it either retreats into familiar contradictions, assumptions, and half-truths of limited perception, or accepts there is a way to

236

♄ Saturn: Spiritual Master, Spiritual Friend

integrate all the contradictory information into an understanding beyond its previous conceptions. It may or may not welcome what and how it must learn to integrate, but because it wants "to know," it suspends many assumptions in trying to find an understanding it can live with. Then it seeks to find commonality in the various ideas and approaches it found that led it to the original crisis of contradictory "truths."

At that point, since all works together to bring about an awareness of the Oneness of Life and Self, our lower mind begins to find ways to integrate all we have learned so our body, feelings, and mind can become a vehicle to attain our aspiration. Along the way we encounter many opportunities to change how we respond to challenges related to any delusions about who we think we are, including the relationship of our lower self to the emerging Higher Self. We also are tested many ways so we may transmute the corrosive doubt of the ego mind which is based in what it believes, but does not know. The path to higher consciousness always leads us beyond belief or doubt into understanding and broadened awareness.

Along the Road of Life, we are offered countless opportunities to view the superstitions of the world with a healthy detachment. Just because many believe something does not make it true. Everything must be examined from many points of view over time to come to a well-rounded, balanced understanding. This relates to Saturn's exaltation in Libra.

As we achieve a holistic view of things, we find ways to see everything with an awareness that, beyond worldly assumptions, there is a state of consciousness which understands how everything is related to everything else. As we continually experience an attunement with the larger field of Loving Light where all are One together, we find we are resolving all lesser karmas and have left behind our prior unhealthy desires and counter-productive exaggerated emotional states. With practice, we diminish any possibility of getting hooked by anger, hatred, pride, the self-grasping, self-cherishing ego-mind, and any

♄ Saturn: Spiritual Master, Spiritual Friend

attachment to forms of enlightenment looking a certain way. At some point we even get beyond being agitated or irritated by the passing things in the world. It all works for our ultimate good, since as we shed the fetters that distract and bind us, we come to an ever-greater awareness of our direct connection with All-That-Is, which accompanies a more constant experience of an ever-increasing sense of Oneness with all of Life.

* * * * * * * * *

Everything we go through, whether pleasurable or painful, can serve to help us stop giving our power to external things in ways that hinder us. The greater the Self-realization of a man or woman, the less they are affected by the phenomenal flux, and the more they experience the whole Universe via a heightened receptivity to the infinite subtle spiritual vibrations in the collective field.

As we grow beyond the power of external difficulties and distractions to hinder us, we become aware that we are not separate from anything within the One Life we all share. We are all part of many spiritual groups, both large and small, and the path to Self-realization always leads us out of separateness through a greater awareness of our Oneness. Then all external things show us our uniqueness and connectedness within the greater Life in which we all play a part necessary to the completeness of the whole.

We have been told by venerable sources we are here to eliminate any sense of separateness existing between us and All-That-Is. This naturally happens as we let go of the limited perceptions of ego-mind with its afflictions and assumptions. In learning to identify with our eternal Self, many things that once plagued us are quickly eliminated.

In becoming strong and clear, we naturally offer what we've learned, assisting other Beings to come out of

238

♄ Saturn: Spiritual Master, Spiritual Friend

suffering, and willingly accept the antidotes offered to us, since we understand we are part of a larger group Soul within the One Life we all share. The healer, the healing, and the healed are ONE. Since everything works as one Life force to bring us to wholeness, from one point of view, you and that which heals you are ONE.

When we are aligned with our Higher Self, we have the power to send out vibrations to attract whatever is beneficial to our highest intention and evolution. Then we enter a conscious dance between the Spiritual world and our ability to steer the process of our evolution, and find we and the God we seek are not separate in any way, shape, or form. If Limitless Light is All-That-Is, and we are individual sentient sparks of Light in a limitless field of Light, then we are never separate from the Omnipresent Source of Light and Life.

Most of us have been taught that Spirit, God or something "higher up in the universe" is looking after us and guiding our footsteps on life's path. However, from another angle the God or Spirit guiding us is not separate from our Highest Self, our individualized Atma-Buddhi-Manas operating at a subtle but very high plane of consciousness. As I offered earlier, the Teacher, the Teaching, and the Taught all exist simultaneously. There is no separation between us and our Highest Self except in the lower self's identification with the parts of us that suffer.

We are Eternity. We have Eternity. We are Time itself. We are evolution. Our "Higher Triad" is our Spiritual Body. This is the source from which all our forms, feelings, and ideas result. Our Highest Self is not separate from the Father-Mother God in Heaven which is ONE. We are the God we seek.

We may be human, but we are simultaneously and indivisibly Eternal Consciousness, a spark of Omnipresent, Omniscient, and Omnipotent Divine Mind. We have more power, wisdom, love, and intelligence than we think. And we will make our Way, Truth, and Light/Life manifest in countless ways across countless lifetimes in the field of Limitless Light which is "All-That-Is."

239

♄ Saturn: Spiritual Master, Spiritual Friend

♄ Saturn: Spiritual Master, Spiritual Friend

About the Author

Robert Wilkinson is a practicing professional astrologer with more than 45 years of experience as a counselor, public speaker, author, publisher, and strategic analyst. With an advanced education in social and humanistic psychology, historical cycles, Eastern philosophies, and spiritual practices, he offers the world a holistic view of the many interrelated things that impact personal and global evolution. He has found that by understanding the patterns of our inner and outer reality, we can find ways to live a more Soulful existence in practical ways, and reclaim our power to become the Loving Wise Intelligence which is our true nature.

He also has been a professional political analyst and a multi-media producer, director, and editor, giving him a wide variety of worldly experiences that help ground the synthesis of philosophical and spiritual approaches he offers in his talks, workshops, classes, and articles. He believes that we all have the power to live our life with intention and purpose, allowing us over time to become the perfect expression of our Higher Self and the living Light of our heart, Soul, and Spirit.

His website Aquarius Papers – Global Astrology (www.aquariuspapers.com) is one of the longest running websites of its kind, offering thousands of articles on a wide variety of astrological, metaphysical, and cultural subjects to visitors from over 130 countries. He is the author of the pioneering work "A New Look at Mercury Retrograde," the first major work on the subject, as well as well as "Love Dad," a grief manual for those who have lost a loved one. He also has other books in development, including one exploring the mysterious mind of cats.

♄ Saturn: Spiritual Master, Spiritual Friend

Made in the USA
Columbia, SC
27 October 2018